WINSPLE : WE INSPIRE PEOPLE

STORIES OF INSPIRING PEOPLE

RAVI GANGANARAS

"Here I bring people around the world to share their inspiring journey which will inspire you to start your own"

Ravi Ganganaras

Contents

Contents

CHAPTER ONE

Alicia Souza

Life into Art

"I don't like to say I have given my life to art. I prefer to say art has given me my life." This is the story of Alicia Souza the famous illustrator and inspiring entrepreneur. Her story starts on 27 January 1987 in the United Arab Emirates. She was the youngest of three siblings, who calls herself the lucky Mistake. Her family was Indian Goan in origin.

Alicia Souza

Education is so important because it makes us capable of what we are. She completed her schooling in UAE. After that, she moved to Australia. In Melbourne, she completed her graduation in Communication Design from RMIT. She stayed in Australia for 5 years.

She wasn't particularly an artist kid. She drew as much as any other kid. Once she scribbled scoter on a wooden partition in their house. She was proud of it, but it probably not looked like the best artistic creation. But she never thought she would do that for her career.

In 2009 she took a leap of faith and moved to India to her roots and co-created Chumbak, one of the most successful brands in India. Before coming to India, Alicia use to work in a bank. It was really scary for her because India was very new and unknown to her. Chumbak was great and never a regretful feeling to her. Because, before that, she never knew how to run a business.

Being an artist and running your own business is not as easy as it sounds. Her life partner's influence on her was important. In 2017 she announced her marriage on a website called the book Began. Her husband's name is George Seemon he is an architect at Stapati. She also published a book called "Dearest George" to express her love story. She is also an animal lover of soul. The sign of that comes out in her work as well.

Alicia Souza has been a freelancer now for almost 10 years. Apart from her solo comics, Alicia has done illustrations for major brands like Google, Yahoo, Infosys, SAP, Times of India, TVS, The Hindu, etc. On her online shop, Alicia stocks posters and tangs that can be downloaded, as well as physical products including calendars, planners, as well as illustrated home decor, and stationery.

Alicia has no formal education in art. This young, vibrant entrepreneur, who was originally hesitant about sharing her artwork online, now has 47,000 followers just on Facebook. Alicia's unapologetically maximalist style, in an era when everything and everyone is trying to be some kind of minimalist, makes her and her work both loveable and relatable. Alicia also has spoken at many events like the Google event in Hyderabad, and a few TEDx talks, at Ink Women among others. According to her, "I think it's legit, when you speak about your work, it becomes more than just paper. I don't think you need it to be more than a paper, as an illustrator, but at the same time, you do."

CHAPTER TWO

Divya Gandotra

Change in Life and Business

"The primary goal is not to make a profit but rather to create value, to change how people do business, perceive things, understand things, or to even change how they live".

Divya Gandotra

Divya Gandotra Tandon is the Founder & Director of Scoop Beats Private Limited. She is also a part of ASTNT Technologies Pvt LTD. She is a young and dynamic entrepreneur, a celebrity manager, a social media manager, and an influential figure. Divya Gandotra Tandon has worked for more than 100 individual stars, influencers, and companies. Hailing from Jammu & Kashmir Divya is currently staying in Noida and pursuing a diploma in computer science and engineering.

    Her journey started as a YouTuber and she has over thirty thousand subscribers on her channel where she reviews and unboxes tech products. "In 2015, everyone in my class was talking about Technical Guruji, that he is making videos and other stuff. I was impressed by his work and at that time I thought why don't I try the same? Everyone will talk about me as well. That was so stupid that I had no idea, that this will be so difficult for me. Being an introvert, I was not good at public speaking, and that problem was reflected in all my videos. But I tried hard to make my level best" recalls Divya. Living in a place like Jammu, which had frequent internet blackouts it was really difficult for Divya to scale up as a YouTuber. She used to make do with a 3G connection exporting videos in 240p. Then in 2016 everything changed. She got a 4G sim card and was finally able to make high-quality videos for her channel. In 2017, she started getting sponsorship and barter units for promotional activities. She also had a good smartphone, a mic, and a laptop to edit.

"Being a YouTuber, I had some bit of knowledge about audience engagement and content creation so I used that knowledge on Facebook and Google as the algorithm was not much different. Constant work helped me a lot."

In April 2018, she created a Facebook page and a website with her friend, which was named The Scoop Beats. And they decided to publish news on websites and memes/videos on Facebook Page. And that's when her entrepreneurial journey began. In the start, Divya and her team used to make inspirational posts so that people would love to share them on their timelines. After that, they started making posts on Facebook that relate to life. They also started making posts on some of the most crucial issues like rape and marital abuse. Their main motive was to make the audience aware of some critical problems in India. She decided to promote democracy, free speech, reliable dissemination of information, and the well-being of its reference groups through her media channels. Her vision is to achieve at least the milestone of 100k subscribers and her goal is to engage audiences and deliver the best content. The company in particular acts as a platform for memes, news, and other viral content. Scoop Beats is an Internet media company. Their aim is to bring their audience to the real world. They do this by delivering information as quickly as possible without compromising the Quality and reliability of Data. They cover topics ranging from technology to science, entertainment, health, and business. The news covered includes both breaking news with universal appeal. In addition, their articles are designed to attract readers' attention and improve retention.

"We are committed to improving the economic, environmental, and social development of the world and boosting entrepreneurship through professionalism, superior quality, and innovation. We strive for excellence and aim to exceed expectations"

At a young age, Divya achieved a lot. She also started a few projects on women's safety and she was also awarded as Entrepreneur Young Achievers award in Delhi and the Incredible Indian icon award in Indore. She is also certified in Fundamental of Digital marketing by Google Unlocked. She learns from the criticism her audience gives her and once said in an interview, "I may not be a good content creator for myself but my audience know me better, they support me and love the content that I create."

CHAPTER THREE

Farrhad Acidwalla

Failure Gives You The Lesson of Success

Farrhad Acidwalla

Farrhad Acidwalla is a 25-year-old entrepreneur, investor, and TEDx speaker. He started as one of the youngest entrepreneurs in the world and is best known as the founder of Rockstah Media and CYBERNETIV

DIGITAL. Acidwalla has been a featured speaker on the TEDx stage, as well as the youngest guest lecturer at IIT Kharagpur's annual entrepreneurship summit. While he still focuses much of his time on Rockstah, Acidwalla also invests in other businesses, such as Consumer Guard, a web-based business he founded with Suhel Seth to handle consumer grievances. Farrhad had an entrepreneurial instinct from a very young age, at the age of 13, borrowed $10 from his parents to build an online community devoted to aviation and aero-modeling. Soon after, he sold that project to a fan for $1,200, and a few years later used $400 to launch Rockstah Media, a business focused on web development, marketing, advertisement, and branding.

Farrhad used to develop blogs and websites for himself which he later sold to different people. And this thought laid the foundation for his first company, Rockstah Media, with an initial investment of $400. He provided the services such as web development, branding, marketing, and advertising to his clients. You may perceive that setting up a company wouldn't have been difficult for Farrhad, as he already had skills and a network. But this was not the case. Farrhad struggled to get the clients on board and also to build a competent team to work with. He had no capital to invest in the fancy infrastructure and to get the experts to work for him. The only thing he had was a sincere idea. Even though he faced numerous rejections, he didn't set back. Instead, he continued to express his entrepreneurial idea, and eventually, it started showing results. The success of Rockstah Media got Farrhad in the spotlight. At 17, he got a chance to feature in a live interview on CNN. Despite the initial struggles, now his company has a team of developers, designers, and marketers worldwide. And his clientele includes National Award winners, corporates, Padma Shree recipients, media personalities, and Public Sector Units. After Rockstah Media's success, Farrhad decided to contribute to the field of cybersecurity and launched his second venture, Cybernetiv Digital.

Acidwalla's most recent brand-building venture took him to the Chenab valley in the Jammu region of Jammu and Kashmir where he was invited by the Indian government to around hundreds of youths. "I reiterated that India is the largest youth population in the world and never before have information, knowledge, and technology been so accessible...My goal was not to just tell them about my story, but to tell them how they can turn their passion into their profession," he said.

Balancing a busy school life with the challenges of running an entrepreneurial venture is a difficult task, one that Farrhad seems to have carried out to perfection. "My main challenges are the paucity of time and trying to multi-task. As a student, I have to dedicate time to my studies and other commitment, which leave me little opportunity for me to indulge in my other work. But thankfully, I have a lot of support from my home, which

I am grateful for," he said.

One of the most crucial pieces of advice by the young achiever is "If you're failing and not learning from it, you're wasting your time. You will learn far more from your smallest failure than you will from your greatest success."

CHAPTER FOUR

Kavita Shukla

The Women of FreshGlow

"The more we can share stories of women entrepreneurs, of people who have walked this path before, who have faced obstacles and have been able to bring their ideas to the world ... it really encourages and inspires young girls and women to think about doing more with their ideas."

Kavita Shukla

Kavita Shukla is the Founder & CEO of The FRESHGLOW Co. and the inventor of FreshPaper, a simple innovation taking on the massive global challenge of food waste. She holds four patents and is a recipient of the biennial INDEX Design to Improve Life Award – the world's largest prize for design. Today, FreshPaper is used by farmers and families across the globe, and The FRESHGLOW Co. has partnered with some of the largest retailers in the world from Whole Foods to Walmart. Kavita has been featured as one of Fast Company's "7 Entrepreneurs Changing the World." She has also been named to the Forbes "30 under 30" list and TIME Magazine's "5 Most Innovative Women in Food."

Kavita's story of simple beginnings, belief, and empowerment has inspired millions worldwide and Hollywood actress and director Bryce Dallas Howard has made a short film inspired by her life. Kavita has spoken about the power of simple ideas at the White House, the United Nations, SXSW, the Global Entrepreneurship Congress, TEDxManhattan, Harvard University, MIT, and Johns Hopkins University. She was also a featured speaker at the Women in the World Summit, along with Hillary Clinton, Angelina Jolie, Meryl Streep, and Oprah Winfrey. At such a young age she has a plethora of achievements and awards behind her all because of a simple home remedy.

Her product started as a middle-school science project which was inspired by her Grandmother's Indian home remedy and soon developed into a world-changing innovation taking on the massive challenge of global food waste. Made from organic spices, FreshPaper is a disposable, recyclable, and biodegradable sheet that naturally keeps producing fresh for longer, therefore, reducing food spoilage. At the age of 13, she created a lab safety device for bottles containing hazardous materials. She patented the device, dubbing it the "Smart Lid." Around that time, she also became interested in the potential uses of fenugreek (Methi) in preserving food and fighting bacterial growth. While visiting her grandparents during a trip to India at age 12, Kavita accidentally drank contaminated water. Her grandmother whipped up a homemade concoction containing ground fenugreek seeds and gave it to her to consume, she took the powder and did not become ill.

"I think I could have never imagined in middle school that today, decades later, I would still be working on that idea, that I would still be working on the same idea I started working on as a little girl. So, I think in many ways that that journey has really defined my career and my life, and it really changed the trajectory of my life."

When she returned home to the United States, Shukla began conducting her experiments with fenugreek, exploring its antibacterial and antifungal properties. Through her research, she found that fenugreek could not only remove toxic substances from aqueous solutions but could also inhibit bacterial and fungal growth. She wondered if this discovery could be applied to food preservation, and had an idea to develop a packaging paper using fenugreek that might better preserve and protect items from bacteria and fungi. She observed that food wrapped in fenugreek-treated paper lasts four to six weeks longer than food protected by traditional wrapping.

It is also natural, non-toxic, biodegradable, and easily produced in large quantities, making it ideal for developing countries and developed nations alike. She obtained a patent for her fenugreek-treated paper in the spring of 2002. This was the birth of her product FreshPaper. In 2010, she founded Fenugreen to market her FreshPaper invention to Farmer's markets and street fairs in Cambridge, Massachusetts Today, Fenugreen is now known as The FRESHGLOW Co.

"Food waste is this massive and very overwhelming challenge, but it's actually something that every single one of us can start to address in our own homes."

CHAPTER FIVE

Ranveer Allahabadia

An Influencer Entrepreneur

"I believe in being an entrepreneur of the self; an entrepreneur is first built in the mind and you have to work your mind and body, and then think about careers, businesses, and other external things."

Ranveer Allahabadia is also known as *BeerBiceps* is a 28-year-old Mumbai-based entrepreneur and content creator who runs the Spotify-exclusive podcast *The Ranveer Show* and has over 2 million subscribers on his YouTube channel. He has also worked with brands such as Amazon Fashion, The Jupiter App, Nurture Farm, Samsung India, RazorPay, BPL India, Gillette India, Cello World, Uniqlo India, upGrad, Men of Platinum, Fitternity, CRED, Alchemlife, Vivo India, Toothsi Aligners, Syska, Great Learning, OK Cupid India, among many others. His content mostly centers on fitness, lifestyle, grooming, motivation, career advice, and entrepreneurship. Ranveer is among one of the best-known influencers in the Indian Social Media community.

Earlier this year, his name was on Forbes' 30 under 30 list which featured 300 young entrepreneurs, leaders, and trailblazers across the Asia-Pacific region, all under the age of 30. These are people who inspire change and drive innovation in their respective fields. After featuring in the list Ranveer talked about achieving his goals in life and said, "I had only 3 goals at the start of my career. 1. A million subscribers on the YouTube channel. 2. A feature on Forbes 30 under 30. 3. To build a unicorn. 2 out of those 3 are now complete. I cried like a baby today. Was pent up for too long. Now on to the next one."

Ranveer Allahabadia

Ranveer came up with the idea of *BeerBiceps* in 2015 as he saw a serious lack of good fitness content in the Indian YouTube scene. His content was one of the first to talk about things like having a balanced fitness instead of being overly obsessed with it. Ranveer always wanted to enter the start-up scenario and saw content creation as a way to enter the market and build his brand. Content creation to him, in the beginning, was just a way to market his start-up. Then as he grew, he realized that it is possible to scale up your YouTube channel, and social media profile and monetize it and treat it like a start-up. Presently, Ranveer has gone back to the start-up that he had in his mind long before accidentally stumbling into being a content creator, "Now, we have gone back to the world of startups, thanks to the clout we have developed over time."

As for the creative process of him and his team, he sees audience feedback in the comments and on social media as the primary driver. He has an internal brainstorming team that runs and manages his channel and who also studies the numbers that his videos are doing constantly. Hence, he and his team stay up-to-date on providing relevant and likable content for his audience. "There is never a shortage of ideas. If at all, there is some sort of creative block, we take a break, travel, and refuel ourselves with creativity." According to him, to be a good and successful content creator, one needs to nail the basics of hardware as well as an out-of-box idea and engaging content. He believes that having good audio is important and much underrated and that good lighting conditions are also very important as these things will make your content more appealing to a wider audience.

On starting his podcasting journey, Ranveer recalls July of 2019. According to him, it was the darkest phase of his mental health and he felt overburdened with responsibilities, exhausted by content creation and the final trigger for him was a very painful breakup. It drove him to the point of considering quitting content creation. Four years of content creation and personal life battles had left him feeling empty and hollow. It was then his partners Viraj Seth and Manish Pandey asked him what he would like to do. Ranveer wanted to do podcasts but then, India did not have much of a podcasting culture. The first few episodes were with friends of his and now he has more than 200 episodes in English and close to 100 in Hindi. The list of guests is never-ending from social media influencers, film stars, spiritual gurus and experts, and academics on various issues everyone has featured on his show. From feeling deflated and dispassionate about content creation, Ranveer created one of the biggest if not the biggest podcasts in India and for him, it is just the beginning.

"Only I know how deflated (and how close to giving up) I was. If I could do it, starting from the lowest point in my life, there's nothing that will stop me from doing it as well! Podcasts are here to stay. Podcasts will change an entire generation of kids."

CHAPTER SIX

Ritesh Agarwal

A Big Business Starts From a Small Idea

In the business world, there's a quotation "A big business starts from a small idea". The same happed with OYO. A council powerhouse, Ritesh Agarwal, always had that study in his mind that he wanted to start a commodity new of his own. It wasn't an easy trip for him, from a small idea to a successful business.

Ritesh Agarwal

Ritesh Agarwal was born in an Indian Marwari family on 16 November 1993. Ritesh's family used to live in Bassam Cuttack, Odisha that time. They used to run a small shop from Rayagada to take care of their family. We can say, that small business helps Ritesh to grow up and establish the multi-billionaire company OYO.

Ritesh completed his early academy education at Sacred Heart School in Rayagada. The business was in his blood from nonage. At the age of 13, he started dealing SIM cards to earn his fund plutocrat. He completed his academic education at St. Johns Senior Secondary academy. After completing his academy life, he moved to, the capital of India, Delhi in 2011 for advanced studies. He wasn't confident about his studies. He wanted to do commodity instigative in his life trip. In the time 2012 Ritesh takes a life-changing decision to drop out of his college education and give 100% focus to his dream.

After dropping out of college, Ritesh started a budget-saving gate for budget hostel reserving. He named his business "Oravel Stays". In 2013 it becomes one of the winners of the Thiel Fellowship program and entered an entitlement of$,000. Ritesh renamed his company OYO in May 2013.

OYO started growing popularly by giving analogous guest gests across the metropolises, to the guests. After its launch, it receives a two-time program from PayPal founder Peter Thiel. In September 2018 it raised$ 1 billion. And in July 2019 Ritesh bought$ 2 billion in shares in his company to increase his stakes.

In 2019, OYO had,000 workers encyclopedically. roughly in India and South Asia, the number was around 8000. also, Ritesh's company set up 26 training institutes for hospitality across India at the end of 2019.

The growth of Ritesh Agarwal's company OYO looks unthinkable. He failed 6times before succeeding in his OYO adventure. According to him "If you hadn't failed. You haven't hardened yourself". He earns numerous achievements in his business life. He was listed in Forbes in the 30 under 30 list for Asia on 27nov 2020. According to Harun rich list 2020, his net worth was roughly$1.1 billion. He's the alternate youthful tone- made billionaire in the world after notorious Kylie Jenner.

Ritesh's trip was successful, as he was determined to achieve his dreams. He'd one thing clear in his mind that he'd to do commodity that was out of the box. He worked day in and day out to achieve it, and in the end, got to the shafts of success.

CHAPTER SEVEN

Sahar Mansoor

Waste-Free

Take care of the beauty of nature for our future. It is our collective and individual responsibility to preserve and tend to the world in which we all live. Sahar Mansoor an enthusiastic environmental activist has seen the greener side to save the mother earth from destruction.

Sahar Mansoor

Sahar completes her school life in 2009. In Sophia High School she was an outstanding student. She won the student of the year award for her outstanding performance in the years 2007 and 2009. After completing her school education, she joins Loyola Marymount University in 2009 for her

B.A. (Bachelor of Arts). She completed her B.A. in 2013 in the subject of Political Science and Environmental Planning. Then she joins the University of Cambridge and complete her M.Phil. in Environmental Economics and law in 2014.

During her studies, she also did some internships. In 2009 she did her first internship with National Geographic. After that, she did another internship with Earth Share in May 2012. She also worked with many institutions. She worked with Heal Africa as a Project Assistance from May 2011 to Nov 2011. She also worked in her college as Resident Advisor. In July 2014 Sahar joins World Health Organization as Mobile Health Researcher. She worked with them till December 2014. After that, she joins SELCO Foundation. She also did Freelance Blog. Her topics in the blog were related to environmental justice, green technology, and environmental policy opinion pieces.

Sahar founded Bare Necessities in the year of 2016. Her reason behind the establishment of Bare Necessities was to achieve a Zero-Waste society. Sahar first learned the concept of Zero-Waste in 2012 while she was an undergraduate student at LMU in Los Angeles. She watched a video of Bea Johnson in her class. Bea Johnson's lifestyle inspires her toward the concept of Zero-Waste.

She revisited the idea in 2014 after coming across Zero-Waste pioneer Lauren Singer's blog. Then 24 years old Lauren was living a waste-free life in New York. After seeing Lauren's life one thought came to Sahar's mind that she and Lauren are the same age, if Lauren can do that, she also can do it too. After that though, she starts more thinking about our trash problem.

To start, Sahar replaced single-use plastic disposables with paper, steel, and bamboo once. Once she ran out of personal products, she learned to make her soap, shampoo, and other products. Now she manufactures these on a large scale through her startup Bare Necessities. She has produced 500gms of waste in the past two years, which she stores in a glass jar.

For her work in changing the narrative on waste in India, Sahar has been recognized by Google India as "The Most Inspiring Indian of the Year." NDTV named her a "Swachh Warrior." MTV India featured her as one of six women re-defining the career paths of the 21st century. She also wins many awards like the 2020 Eco-Star of Asia, Young Leader Award, 40 under 40 Award, UnLTD Entrepreneur Award 2019, etc.

Sahar has no intention of preaching to people how they should live. But for those who care about the environment, she says this is the perfect place to get started. "It looks much harder than it is. If you care about your environmental impact - you should give it a shot. You can start by taking baby steps and slowly transitioning your lifestyle. "It's not time-consuming, it's not expensive and it's not just for granola hippie people. Your grandmother was probably a zero waster."

CHAPTER EIGHT

Sreelakshmi Suresh

Wonder Girl

"Success is not an accident, it is hard work, perseverance, learning, studying, sacrifice, and most of all, the love of what you are doing or learning to do." Sreelakshmi Suresh, a girl who is the first female youngest entrepreneur as the youngest Web Designer & world's youngest Chief Executive. Sreelakshmi was born on 5th February 1998. Her family was from Kozhikode, Kerala, India. Her father's name is Mr. Suresh Menon; he is a lawyer at the Calicut Bar Council. Her mother Mrs. Viju Suresh is a school teacher. Without their encouragement and love, Sreelakshmi couldn't reach her success.

Sreelakshmi Suresh

She completed her schooling at Presentation Higher Secondary school in Kerala. Further, she completed her graduation in Business Management from St. Joseph's College in Devagiri.

Sreelakshmi began using computers when she was just 3 years old. Her interest in computers and technology was extreme. She started designing one year later at the age of 4. Finally, she successfully designed her website at the age of 6.

At the age of 8 Sreelakshmi when she was in class 4, she designed a website for her school. Impressed by her work, the forest minister of the Kerala state government Mr. Vinay Viswam came to inaugurate the website on 15 January 2006. After that, she wanted to start things on her own. So, she launched her start-up in 2009. The name of the start-up was "eDesign". Then she started her next company "Tiny Logo" at the age of 11.

Sreelakshmi also manages another company, "Online Pixel", through which she impacts knowledge to the needy. She also designed a website for the Bar Council of Kerala. Currently, she is working as the CEO of eDesign.

Sreelaksmi Suresh is an exceptionally talented Web Designer and Entrepreneur. She has received several awards for her contributions to the web design field. In 2008, she received the National Award for Exceptional Achievement from the Ministry of Women and Child Development. The award was presented to her by Sonia Gandhi on 5th January 2009 at Vigyan Bhavan, New Delhi.

She also received many national and international awards for her excellence. Like Golden Web Award (USA), Sixty Plus Education Award (CANADA), Feeble mind's Award of Excellence (UK), Webmasters Ink Award (USA), Watashi Science Movement Excellence Award 2007 (INDIA), Moms Global Award for inspirational Website 2006-2007 (UK), ProFish-N-Sea- Charters World Class Website Award (BRAZIL), etc. Not only this but she was also selected by Info-group as a brand ambassador.

Sreelakshmi has designed and developed about 100+ Websites, some of which are also covered by the Media. The famous English Channel in India, Times Now also featured her on their program named "Amazing Indians" in 2012. She gained recognition and fame in 2006. Since then, she has received huge attention and appreciation for her work. Now she is an inspiration for youth and an epitome of creativity and talent.

Sreelakshmi Suresh is now a well-known web designer and entrepreneur. Her hard work, consistency, and perseverance are the reasons behind her success and recognition. So, if you want something in your life, don't wait for the right time. Try to make this your right time.

Reshmi Daga

Satisfy Your Hunger

Some people dream about success, while other people get up every morning and make it possible. Reshmi Daga not just dreams about her success She works hard to make it the reality of her life. Reshmi Daga was born in 1980 in a typical Marwari family. Reshmi's family used to live in a small town called Ramgarh in West Bengal. There were four members in her family. Her mother, father, and her brother. With her family, she shifted to Delhi when she was just 6 years old. The upbringing and love of her family were essential in way of her successful journey.

Reshmi Daga

Swami Vivekananda says "The secret of life is not enjoyment but education through experience." Reshmi's education life was important for making her business life joyful. After finishing school life, she joined the Delhi College of Engineering in 1997. She finished her B.E, Electrical Engineering course in 2001. Then she joined the Indian Institute of Management Ahmedabad for MBA and completed her MBA in 2003.

Entrepreneurship, nevertheless, wasn't the first step for Reshmi. After completing her MBA, she took up a job at IBM through campus recruitment in June 2003. After the first few months of training, she was given a sales manager role, where she learned her greatest life skills. After that, she joined Johnson & Johnson in December 2005 as a regional sales executive. There she experienced working with doctors, chemists, and parents. In December 2007 she left Johnson & Johnson. After that, she gets married and moved to Bangalore with her husband. After moving to Bangalore, she joined a Bangalore-based ed-tech start-up company TutorVista January 2008.

In 2011, she started her first start-up at Afday.com. It was an e-commerce platform for jewelry, home decoration, and gift articles from artists across the country. After one year Rashmi realized it would not go far. So, she decides to shut down that business. After that, she joined Bluestone an online jewelry store and worked with them till Oct 2013. After leaving Bluestone she joined OLA in Dec 2013 for 8 months as sales head. Her thought behind working in multiple sectors was, that will make her prepare for a much bigger landscape later. It happened in July 2014.

In 2014 she moved to the food industry with FreshMenu. FreshMenu is an online restaurant that today clocks 14,000 orders per day from its app and website across Bangalore, Mumbai, South Delhi, and Gurugram. And the average order amount is Rs.320. They have 1,800 different food items from different food cuisine. According to Rashmi Daga FreshMenu does everything, from sourcing the ingredient to getting food delivered to the customer's table.

For her impressive work as an entrepreneur, she gets many awards. She was awarded Forty under 40 in 2018 by Et & Spencer Stuart. She gets ET Facebook Women Ahead Award in Aug 2018. As a women entrepreneur, she received Et Prime Women Award in April 2019. In Aug 2019 she received Fortune 40 under 40 by Fortune.

Her journey was not easy. From a sales manager post to a founder of a successful business. In this way, she faced many experiences, good as well as bad. Throughout her journey, in every step, she learned new things. That helps her to achieve fame of success. So never stop learning, because life never stops teaching.

CHAPTER TEN

Suumit Shah

Dukan Of Success

Suumit Shah

Suumit Shah is the Founder and CEO at Dukaan App. A DIY (Do It Yourself) platform that enables merchants with zero programming skills to set up their e-commerce store using smartphones. The platform was launched in just over 48 hours, and millions of merchants have since started selling online using the app. Dukaan began monetizing in early May 2020 and earned its first revenue of over $44K in 30 days. In October, just four months after starting, Dukaan raised $6 million (Rs 44 crore). Dukaan app currently has more than 150,000 stores, with more than 500,000 products added to 40 different categories of businesses. The app covers more than 400 cities and has received more than 75,000 orders. In short, the app is helping to make a huge impact across the country. ``We offer Desi Bharosa with world-class technology, we believe that through a platform like Dukan we can create a digital India," says Suumit.

Born in 1990, Suumit hails from a middle-class family. After completing his schooling, he used to work in his uncle's shop in Satara, Maharashtra. He completed his engineering at a college in Sangli, another small city in Maharashtra, and then came to Mumbai in search of job opportunities. Suumit enrolled in computer hardware and networking course. Suumit started working professionally with online realty firm Housing as a digital marketing manager in 2014. Over the next few years, he went on to work for TinyOwl and founded two startups—RiseMetric, a digital marketing agency, and Rankz, a content marketing platform. Suumit met Subhash Chaudary who is currently Dukaan's CTO during his computer course and both of them had an eye for digital marketing. They soon partnered to start a marketing agency called Risemetric. After running the agency successfully, they both launched Dukaan App in May 2020. Dukaan was arguably innovative and became a successful start-up within no time.

The idea of Dukaan came up because of COVID-19 and the subsequent lockdown which was imposed. Suumit and Subash noticed that the imposition of lockdown across India led small and medium-sized shopkeepers to shut their businesses. However, big companies still managed to keep their businesses open. It was small retailers whose businesses had to suffer losses and then close down. To aid these retailers in this crisis was the idea behind Dukaan. The process of signing up with Dukaan is simple, "Even a person with zero tech background could do it," according to Suumit. The shopkeepers needed to sign up on the app, they would get an OTP (one-time-password), then they could write the name of their business and start adding all products. Every seller would get a unique link where they would be able to display whatever they are selling.

But as we further dive into the story of Dukaan it gets even more interesting. On one of the lockdown mornings last April, Suumit got a WhatsApp message from an anonymous number. The sender happened to be one of the local retail store owners from Indiranagar, Bengaluru, who was desperately trying to sell Jockey underwear in a PDF format. "Here's the list of items we are selling. Please have a look at the PDF and let me know which one you want to buy," read the message. Suumit was baffled at the fact that the poor shopkeeper was using a primitive method to sell his products. "Why doesn't he have an eCommerce store?" Suumit wondered.

This made Suumit have even more questions in his mind. How would he be keeping track of all orders? What if an order comes from outside Bengaluru? "WhatsApp doesn't give any service for geotargeting kind of feature," he wondered. His curiosity made him explore the pain points of small businesses. And then came the idea: *"Ek simple solution banate hain"* (Let's make a simple solution). The plan was to enable offline merchants to come online, and the product was Dukaan, which Shah rolled out last June along with Subhash Choudhary.

Through the story of Dukaan, we can understand how an entrepreneurial mind works. Dukaan's excellence and success is in its simplicity. We can see how a curious and inquisitive mind can create ideas that can solve even the most precarious problems.

CHAPTER ELEVEN

Tilak Mehta

The Wonder Boy :

Age is just a number and maturity is a choice. Young boy Tilak Mehta is the perfect example of this quote. In 2006 Tilak was born in this human world. His family was a typical Indian Gujarati family from Aurangabad, Maharashtra. His father, Mr. Vishal Mehta, was a bank manager. His mother, Mrs. Kajal Mehta is a housewife. He also has a younger sister named Tanvi Mehta. The importance of his family in his life was great. That helps him become an entrepreneur from a normal boy.

His journey in the business world starts on a vacation. He went on a vacation to his uncle Ghanshyam Parekh's house. He returned home the next day. He left his math book at his uncle's house. But he needed that book urgently because of his exam. At that time, he was in class 8.

TILAK MEHTA

His father arrived home late that day. He was tired and not in the position to bring the book to his son. Tilak asked his father about taking the book back from his uncle's house through the courier. But the courier charges for the same day are as high as the book price.

This was the turning point where the idea came into my mind of Tilak. He thinks if we start our logistics and provide the courier at a reasonable rate then it can help many people. From his simple thought, the beginning of Paper-N-Parcel started.

Initially, he started by himself and delivered the courier in his way. Then after some time, he joins the dabbawalla with his team and takes the orders and supplies the orders to the needy customers. The system is as if the dabbawalla shifts the courier from the sender to the receiver destination, they get commission-based on the range he covers or traveled.

The Paper-N-Parcel was initially providing the services only in Mumbai city. He divides Mumbai into 60 circles to give good service. Tilak's net worth crossed 100 Crores Rupees from only his smart idea. The number is increasing day by day as speedily spreading this company.

He becomes Indian Youngest Entrepreneur in India. He archives and provides a parcel with a minimum price which proves age is just a number. At the age of 16, he manages his study and his company Paper-N-Parcel.

He wins the "Young Entrepreneur" title at the India Maritime Awards in 2018. He is the youngest recipient of the Forbes Leadership Award. He received the Global Child Award in January 2020 for entrepreneurship. He is also a speaker at TEDx.

Tilak Mehta not only inspires budding entrepreneurs but also many parents who should support their children's ideas and dreams ignoring all the odds and negativity. Any child who is curious about knowing and learning new things about everything can be the next young entrepreneur of India.

CHAPTER TWELVE

Ikshita Tewari

Spy of Healthy Food

Life is 10% what happens to us and, 90% how we react to it. Ikshita Tiwari is a great reactor in her life. She was born in an Indian typical family in Lucknow, Uttar Pradesh. She completed her schooling in 2011 at La Martiniere girls college. At the age of 10, one day in her school classroom, one teacher asked her what career she want to pursue, and her answer was different from others. She was the only person in the class of 30, who aspired to be a spy.

Ikshita Tewari

At school at first, she was in the science stream. Due to less interest in science, she left that stream. Her favorite subject was English and Political Science. After completing their school life, she joined St. Stephens College in Delhi in the year 2011. She completed her Bachelor's Degree in Political Science and Economics in 2014. After that, she joined University College Dublin in Ireland for her Master's Degree. She completed her Muster's Degree in International Relations and Affairs in the year 2015.

Ikshita starts her work life at the age of 15. An event management company had hired her to talk to the crowd and make them participate in brand-related activities. With no experience in the field, she nervously switched on the mic on a stage. After that, her instinct took over and she rocked the stage. In 2013 she worked with Times Group as an Intern Reporter. Her news zone was the New Delhi city section. During that time, she published articles on crime, education, and the topic of environment beat. After that, she did another internship with Junior Chamber International as International Officer. Then in June 2015, she joined SuperValu in Sales and Crime Outreach.

After SuperValu, She Joined Envoc Communications Consulting. She worked in Envoc first as an Associative Consultant, then as a PR Consultant. In January 2020, she joined ISHO as Marketing Communication Lead. Now she is the President of Retail and Trade at the Women's Indian Chamber Of Commerce and Industry (WICCI). WICCI is an international organization that boosts and builds entrepreneurship and businesses through greater engagement with government, institutions, and global trade networks.

In May 2018, she founded Nutriplate India. The idea of Nutriplate India came up in her mind in between her weight loss journey. She was not alone in the process; her mother was with her. Nutriplate India is a homegrown business that offers a wide range of breakfast cereals, healthy namkeens, and mixtures made out of millets, seeds, and other superfoods, granola, and seeds nourishment balls, millet breakfast flakes, and high protein diabetic atta. Their cooked products include burgers, wraps kebabs, salads bowls, and some Indian meals.

Ikshita Tiwari's Nuriplate India is a great success in the market for healthy food. The seven-member start-up which has been completely digital so far no plans to make its presence in retail stores.

Rajshree Panse

A warrior is born through the mind:

Rajshree Panse

A warrior is born through the mind Rajshree's life could have been a perfect example of a housewife who was married at 21 until she decided against it. Rajashree, due to some financial problems was married at 21 to a man who was hardly compatible with her. She was ridiculed and even beaten by her then-husband before deciding that she had had enough and thus resulting in her filing for a divorce. Her companion at the point was her sorrow and her two daughters who were far too young to understand the storm that was swirling through her life. Rajshree was unemployed at this point in her life battling financial crisis yet again and rippling depression. She was a marketing executive but due to her regressing mental health issues, she had to leave her then marketing job and venture into a long and tedious legal battle.

This was the Flashback she had on the day her life completely changed. Rajshree was nominated for a Padma Vibhusan for her contribution to the field of mental health. Upon hearing this good news from her daughter, she went on a little trip down her memory lane to rediscover her path back. In a time when even living was a tedious job for Rajshree, she had the dare to dream. Dream of a better life for herself and her daughters. Things were difficult for Rajshree until she found herself working as an assistant for a lifestyle and financial coach, where she read all the books to her heart's content that were available in the library. She initially managed social media and appointments for her boss but slowly yet steadily she managed to train herself in the works of life and money coaching.

A point in her life suddenly appeared thereafter, when Rajshree faced a sudden occurrence in her life. She noticed that wherever she would go or whatever she would do, she came into contact with the number 11. From the views in her youtube videos or any bus she might be traveling or any picture she might be enjoying, she saw the number 11. Upon researching and finding out more about this phenomenon she was experiencing, she came to know about angel numbers and lightworkers. She believed that this was the universe's way of communicating with her and guiding her to a path of service and positivity towards various people who are not very fortunate.

Talking about her purpose in life, she told Winsple that she found out through meditation and self-actualization that, she has found her calling. Her calling is to engage with people and live a life of freedom and service to others and that is why she became a life coach. Life coaching is not only a profession for Rajshree, it is a way of life. Telling people how to live their life is not the goal of Rajshree, helping them to find out their passion and purpose in life and guiding them to build a life around them is the main intention of Rajshree's work.

When she found out about the news of her being nominated for the second-highest civilian award in our country, Rajshree felt elated yet grounded at the same time. She looked back into the time when she wandered on this earth, purposeless and suffering, tied down to her mind and societal expectations. She thought of her journey of becoming a woman of valor and courage and vision. She realized that she has always been one, just below the surface, like a phoenix rising from the ashes of her past self into the bright light.

Rajshree has now become an example and a role model which growing up she sought but didn't have. She has broken the barriers that stopped her, cut the weight that pulled her down, and learned how to fly, but the best part is that she has taught many more of her clients to do the same with their life. Rajshree Panse as we speak is probably changing her life for the better in the process of changing her student.

How to find Rajshree Panse:

Instagram: https://www.instagram.com/lifestyle_coach_rajshreepanse/

LinkedIn: https://www.linkedin.com/in/authorandlifestylecoachrajshreepanse/

Facebook: https: //www.facebook.com/rajshree.panse/

CHAPTER FOURTEEN

Neelam Sarda

Towards True Equality

Neelam Sarda

Mrs. Neelam Sarda is a social activist who works to spread awareness and reduce the stigma around menstruation and menstrual products. She is situated in Chennai city and has worked for many years in this field. She promotes and creates awareness for the use of sustainable products for menstruation. Her journey toward this initiative started at home with her daughter. She recalls that she has always been a parent who has been open towards talking about everything with their child she was open with her daughter about periods from the very beginning. Despite of that when her daughter started her periods she had even more questions about the subject. This got her thinking that if her daughter has a plethora of questions then what about those who do not have access to the right mediums and the right literature about the matter.

That was just the beginning of her journey as a social worker who worked towards menstrual awareness. Even before that Neelam had been working as a social worker arranging Saree banks (wherein people donated sarees and over 50,000 sarees were distributed to those who were in need), village help drives working with Kiran Bedi, the former Lt. Governor of Puducherry. Neelam is also a holder of several records. One of her records is of installing the highest number of vending machines, 3000, all over India. All of these machines were for dispensing sanitary pads. Another record that she holds is for the highest number of biodegradable sanitary napkins distributed in a day, wherein she distributed about 22,000 sanitary napkins in a day in Chennai.

As an activist who works for menstrual awareness, she talks about how to reduce the stigma and shame which is associated with periods in our society. According to her, the change must come within the structure of our family, and it is the women who must resist the stigma and the shame. It is the girls who are going through their periods who need to educate as well as call out such old-fashioned behavior. Neelam talks about a condition known as premenstrual syndrome which is a result of the social stigmatization of menstruation. It is because of this and the restrictions which are put on girls when they are menstruating that cause hormonal and psychological problems in their bodies before their menstrual cycle begins which can have detrimental effects on their health. The only way Neelam says, we can battle this is by educating and normalizing the idea of menstruation within our family and further within society.

She talks about the male figures in her life especially her father who was a doctor. Neelam mentions how her father was the one who normalized the idea of menstruation to her. She recalls the time when she got her first period and her father who was not at home then left her a letter with a diagram explaining to her the whole process. Her father was very open with her and so was her brother and when she got married even her husband was very supportive of her so much so that Neelam's line of menstrual cups called *Pride* was launched by her husband under his company's banner. Hence, she says for change to happen in the perception of menstruation and its normalization, family plays a major role.

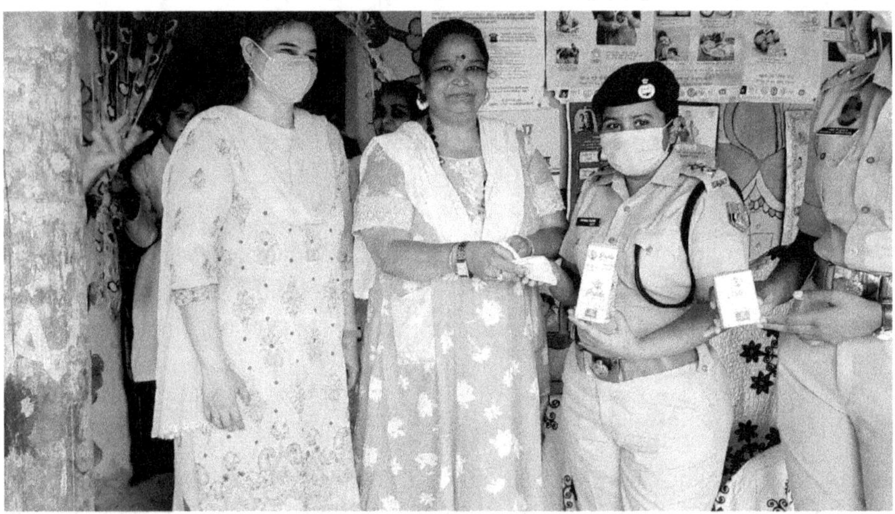

Along with creating awareness around normalizing menstruation, Neelam also believes in green menstruation. She is a big promoter of menstrual cups which in comparison to sanitary pads, which are the most common products used by women in India during periods, are more eco-friendly. She talks about how sanitary pads are made of non-biodegradable materials and are not reusable. Menstrual cups on the other hand can be used for up to 5 years and are a much healthier option. She says that the gel inside the sanitary pads can be harmful to the vagina and cause infections while the cup has no such materials in it. Menstrual cups are also an economical option as each sanitary pad is only good for use for a short period of time and they cost from Rupees 3 to 10 individually, the cost of sanitary pads is high whereas a cup is much cheaper. Therefore, she concludes that a menstrual cup is much more beneficial than a sanitary pad in all three ways: ecological, health, and financial. Neelam has conducted almost a hundred workshops under her banner in the past 5 years and distributed more than 1600 menstrual cups along the way.

10:24

Hindi ePaper, EPaper D...
epaperm.patrika.com

अनम्यूट के तहत मासिक धर्म स्वास्थ्य संबंधी कार्यशाला

चेन्नई. 'शास्त्रा' आईआईटी मद्रास द्वारा अनम्यूट कैम्पेन के अंतर्गत माहवारी के दौरान स्वच्छता के लिए एक कार्यशाला का आयोजन किया गया। यह कार्यशाला टी. नगर स्थित चूडर स्वयंसेवी संस्था द्वारा चलाए जा रहे प्रशिक्षण शिविर के तहत आयोजित की गई जिसमें 12 से 22 साल तक की लड़कियों ने भाग लिया।

कार्यशाला में मासिक धर्म स्वास्थ्य विशेषज्ञ नीलम सारडा ने मासिक धर्म के विभिन्न उत्पादों और उस दौरान अपने स्वास्थ्य पर ध्यान रखने संबंधी जानकारी दी। साथ ही उनको आने वाले समय में पर्यावरण की सुरक्षा और मासिक धर्म उत्पादों विशेषकर पर्यावरण संरक्षण के लिये मेंस्टूअल कप के विशेष प्रयोग के बारे में भी समझाया। इस अवसर पर चूडर संस्था के पदाधिकारी भी उपस्थित थे।

Finally, her message to all the people is that equality can only come when there is a change in mentality. She is a firm believer in 'change begins at home. She says that it is only when men start to respect women and vice versa in terms of their work, their opinions, their life, and their bodies only then can we achieve equality and modernity in its true sense. According to her, being modern is not about what kind of clothes you wear or what kind of language you speak, the true essence of modernity and equality lies in respecting each other and being open towards each other, sharing and discussing with our children and elders the problems of our bodies and normalizing speaking to each other about it rather than making it a matter of shame. She also urges that everyone should try to adopt Green menstruation and start making a shift toward menstrual cups for a clean and green future.

CHAPTER FIFTEEN

Sapna Kumar

AN OPTIMISTS WAY OF LIFE

Sapna Kumar

It is said that God helps those who help themselves, such as in the story of Mrs. Sapna Kumar. Throughout her life, she has held her head high and helped everyone around her, and spearheaded her problems. Life has not been easy for Mrs. Kumar, being born in a traditional Punjabi family where boys had more freedom than girls. She rebelled against the patriarchal structure of her family but to no heed, becoming a rebel without a cause. At that age, all of us are looking for answers and she tried to find hers in the Bhagavad Geeta, which she had overheard her elders talk about. While spirituality played an important role in the latter part of her life, at this point in time the philosophy of Geeta was beyond her use as it did not give a solution to her rebellion. Being a happy-go-lucky girl who had done everything to resist the structure she now tried to find ways in which she could be happy in what was defined to her. If we really think about it, life is like this a lot of times. Sometimes it happens to be so that, things do not go our way or they remain out of our control and we feel powerless. It is in those moments we should remember to find happiness in little things and fleeting moments as it helps us get through the sadness which we feel.

As she grew older, she got married while completing her studies and is still happily married, as she quips about her happy marriage, "where she is happy and he is married!" Through her years of marriage, she raised two upstanding, well-mannered, and respectful children, a girl and a boy, both of whom are now grown up. As a young parent, she learned a lot from her children, in a way growing up with the,m and finally when the older one turned eighteen, M.rs Sapna decided it was high time she started to work on herself.

It is never two too late in life, even after raising two children, Mr.s Sapna was able to work on herself. Her motto became "18 till I die" which made her feel young and energetic. She made a strict routine for herself and moved towards a healthy way of life. Even though she had no formal degrees to her name she educated herself in various skills such as Vastu Shastra, premonition, intuitions, color therapy, numerology, astrology, motivating people, counseling, predictions, communications, holistic health, yoga, kundalini you, body language to name a few. What motivated her through all of this was a proverb heard through times, "A healthy body inhabits a healthy mind." Mrs. Kumar has made predictions that have come true as well, an instance which she recollects is the 2004 Indian General Elections where she had predicted Dr. Manmohan Singh to become the Prime

Minister and P. Chidambaram to be the Finance Minister of the country. Apart from dabbling in astrology and spirituality she also is a writer. She has been writing motivational articles and quotes, poems, and much more and publishing them on the internet since 2000 when she started to use the World Wide Web.

Another one of her skills has been counseling people. She has helped multiple people throughout their life journeys and even saved some from taking their lives. She recalls an instance where once she ran into a woman who was sobbing on the street wanting to end her life. The woman dashed into Mrs. Sapna and shouted "I can't take it anymore it's useless no one cares for me, whom should I live for?" Mrs. Sapna took her home made her a cup of tea and gave her suggestions on how to get her life back on track and how to stay positive in the face of adversity.

The woman to this day thanks Mrs. Sapna and is grateful to her for her efforts in saving her life. In another instance which she recalls, a friend of hers had stopped eating after some complications developed after giving birth. Sapna made her porridge and slowly motivated her to eat little by little, nursing her back to health with her kind, selfless and inspiring effort. Mrs. Sapna also has directed her efforts to work for numerous NGOs to give and serve those who cannot do it themselves. She has been associated with an adoption center taking care of children from ages 0-5 years. She tells the story of a blind boy who had been adopted by an overseas couple but when he was adopted he was not blind and as soon as he developed the condition he was sent back by the couple.

After getting to know his plight Mrs. Sapna shared his case papers from the orphanage with a doctor. It was discovered that the boy had a genetic condition and would not be able to recover from the blindness making her wonder if that was the reason the couple sent the boy back and if they would have done so if the child was their own. This broke Mrs. Sapna's heart but the matrons in the orphanage assured her that this was a common case and the boy will be taken to a shelter for the blind nearby where he will be taken care of properly. She also recalls how the matrons in the orphanage worked tirelessly putting up a smile on their faces providing for the children selflessly and how their faces would light up when Mrs. Sapna brought gifts for them.

Despite all of this Mrs. Sapna's life has not been one without its lows. She was hit with depression and for a good 10 years, she fought with it. It became difficult for her to get out of bed and find joy in things. She fought with those who loved her and felt like nothing mattered around her. It was a time when she felt helpless and the cries in her head asked why isn't anyone helping her? She felt as if she could not talk to anyone, afraid of being judged. Finally, she decided to seek help from her daughter who was a psychologist. Her daughter without judgment helped her get through the difficult phase in her life. Her daughter's counseling had given her a new motto: "I challenge the worst in me and compete with the best in myself."

A woman who is fond of reading, writing, exploring new things, and meeting new people, Mrs. Sapna has come a long way in her life. The once confusing philosophy of the Bhagavad Geeta now makes sense to her and has become the guiding light in her life. She is an example of remaining determinant and making one's pathways towards happiness. We can learn from her how one can work towards building a connection with the community through selfless actions and how having an iron-strong will can make one progress in life. Mrs. Sapna is an optimist who is grateful for God and the gift of life which is given to her.

Amita Kapoor

LEARNING THROUGH ACCEPTANCE:

Amita Kapoor

Life is about perspective. If we have it in us to look at things from a positive perspective we can change even the most morose situations for the better. Mrs. Amita Kapoor is an author and a Mother. Her book *My Son My Guru: Sunshine beyond the Clouds,* is about her and her son, who was born with Down syndrome. The book encapsulates her journey has been in raising a special child. The name of her book is what signifies hope for a better tomorrow. She says that beyond every cloud there is sunshine waiting for us, we just need to persevere through the difficult times and a better world is out there waiting for us. And such has been her journey. During the initial years after her son Abhishek's birth, she did not realize that her son will become her Guru but as time passed she realized and accepted her and her son's situation and tried to make the best out of it.

"Our journey should be from hopelessness to hopefulness. No matter what I am not going to give up."

An instance she recalls is when her son was born. She was lying down and she had asked the doctor to put her son on her chest as she had heard from somewhere that doing so strengthens the bond between the mother and her child. It was after the doctor had placed her son on her chest, that she remembers one of the doctors saying, "I think he is a downs child." At that point in time, she did not know what it meant but as she got to know what it meant and what Down syndrome is, she admits being clueless about how to raise a special child. It was then her pediatrician wrote to her a prescription for life', to raise her child not differently, not make her son feel different from others.

It took Amita two years to accept the fact that her son was a special child and she says that this is what started her journey towards making an effort toward her son. Her family shifted from Delhi to Pune because it was a smaller city and her son would have the company of other relatives there. Children with Down syndrome she mentions learn better through observations as opposed to conventional methods of teaching her son Abhishek learned and observed a lot in Pune and she put him in a school for Special children where he spent 23 years. Amita believes that children should not be compared to each other especially in the Down syndrome category as it may cause certain complexes. She advises parents to let them live freely and do whatever they can to the best of their abilities. She talks about Abhishek's qualities of dancing and being able to introduce himself and his life experiences concisely.

"A lot of people ask me why to have I written *My Son My Guru*, but that is the fact. That is the learning I have taken from him, and I have to give him credit."

Throughout her life, she recalls how her son taught her many things. She recalls the time when her husband passed away in 2010. It was a very difficult time for her and her family and she was worried about how her son will handle the loss. Amita says that during that period the school Abhishek went to, he would gather all the children there to the place where they did the prayers and asked all the children to pray for his deceased father. That was his way of getting over the loss and he even taught Amita how praying will help her find closure as well. Her son always prays before every meal no matter where he is and she says that it was because of this she learned gratitude.

She says that wherever she has reached now and whatever has been her journey over the past 36 years it is a result of the love and support and she is grateful to each and every person involved in the journey. It was in fact her son's nature that made her realize that she needed to be thankful to the universe for what she has achieved. She says that her whole journey of 36 years has been filled with moments and realizations such as these that is why she keeps on repeating, *My Son My Guru.*

Finally, she shares her delightful experience of the successful launch of her book which motivated and touched many parents and children. Amita further throws light on her career as a life enrichment coach and how people should enrich their lives and the days they are blessed with. She advises people on a way to enrich their lives by bringing a smile to the faces of others and giving them the gift of hope. She believes that there is no one general advice that she can give which would fit everyone, rather she says that everyone's life and journey are different, and as the bad times come one should face them bravely and with courage, and the outcome will always be good. She asks people to give their hundred percent in their tasks whether it is at home or office. According to her "My Journey would have been impossible without the unconditional love and support of my complete family. They all stood by me at all times to give Abhishek so much care, and love and supported me in every way."

Amita's journey can teach us the importance of keeping a positive attitude and an open mind. If she did not look at her situations optimistically and did not develop an accepting attitude she would not have been able to come such a long way. It is important that we learn about the journeys of people like Amita and Abhishek who have overcome stigmas in order to learn from them and move forward with our own journeys.

CHAPTER SEVENTEEN

Arpita Sarda

MAKING THE LEADERS OF TOMORROW BY TELLING STORIES OF THE
LEADERS FROM THE PAST

Arpita Sarda

Since our childhood, we hear stories of heroes, yet there are so many
whose stories remain unsung. The real-life leaders and heroes whose acts of
valor from which we can inspire ourselves and our life. Ms. Arpita Sarda is
an entrepreneur who has started the Kreative Kids Klub, a platform where

children from age six to thirteen can come and learn from the stories of these great sung and unsung heroes. The aim of the start-up is simple; to groom kids so that they can become leaders of the future with character, competence, and confidence.

Arpita really enjoys being with the children, teaching them, and interacting with them. Before starting Kreative Kids Klub, Arpita used to take tuition classes for children but then shifted to a corporate job. During her corporate days, she realized that teaching was her passion all along and it is after that she decided to start the Kreative Kids Klub. She started Kreative Kids Klub during the COVID-19 lockdown in 2020 with her 13-year-old son Naman who helped her set up the online classes for the children.

She tells the story of how her son Naman woke up early in the morning with his dad to see the US Presidential debate between Joe Biden and

Donald Trump. That is when Arpita found out that her son had an interest in learning about leaders; what they say and believe in, and stories of these leaders with their qualities. Although she is an engineer by profession, Arpita considers History to be really close to her heart. She started to tell both her children the stories of the leaders and then during the lockdown she approached her son if they could make it an initiative involving other children. During the early days of the lock, Arpita recalls being tired and unhappy and not being able to give her 100% to anything. It was then she and her son started to work towards Kreative Kids Klub and her son had suggested from his experience of online classes to make these sessions interactive with quizzes, games, and so on. And since then, Arpita has not looked back.

Children from ages 6-13 can come and participate in the storytelling sessions and learn about the leaders and heroes of the nation as well as work on their reasoning skills and play interactive games. The primary focus is to build the correct attitude and a strong aptitude. In the sessions, Arpita also makes sure that the events which happen in the leader's lives are relatable to them in their personal lives. Arpita shares the story of Arun Khetarpal, a 21-year-old soldier, who fought in the 1971 Indo-Pak war and was martyred in the battle of Basantar. He lost his life, choosing to serve the nation through the army even though he was selected by IIT, one of the premier institutions in India. He was awarded the Paramveer Chakra, an honor bestowed upon brave soldiers by the Indian government, and was the youngest at the time to receive the award.

Years later, Arun's father had gone to Pakistan and he met the officer who had ended his son's life. He was told how his son fought bravely in the battle and it was a proud moment for him as the enemy praised his son's bravery and valor. According to Arpita, Such stories inspire us to be better leaders and work towards the betterment of the community. From such stories, children inculcate a sense of gratitude and learn qualities like bravery and selflessness, which are important for being good leaders. She also shares an instance where one parent of a Kreative Kids Klub student told her that from the classes he had understood that nothing is impossible, everything is possible with enough hard work and dedication. And when Arpita hears such instances she feels like her small initiative has been successful in serving its purpose.

Arpita believes that one shouldn't be strict with the children, even though she conducts online classes, she has never forced the children to keep their videos on or talk during the class. She says there are times when the children are not in the mood to keep their videos on and they do not want to interact especially in the initial few classes but as the classes go on they keep their videos on, interact and ask questions. It's a slow but long-lasting process. Children in the classes are eager to pass on the information they have learned and do not have a problem with the slightly longer, one and a half to two-hour duration of the classes. The classes are structured such that, she tells the story of a great leader first after which every child tells whatever qualities they learned & liked from the story and then they move on to solving logical reasoning questions and finally they all play a game.

Arpita recalls that the children are the most excited about playing games. On Sundays, the children usually present what they have learned throughout the sessions and it is her young son, Naman who conducts these Sunday sessions. Children feel very connected to Naman bhaiya. Arpita's passion for teaching and her love for the children is what has been the spirit of Kreative Kids Klub, where she is grooming children to be great leaders of tomorrow. Arpita has also been selected for IIM-Nagpur's Women Entrepreneurship program where she will learn to grow her initiative and reach many more young leaders of tomorrow.

Mugdha Yelkar Kekre

Cities far far away

Mugdha Yelkar Kekre

I have always wondered - is entrepreneurship a latent switch? Does it exist in everyone who gets switched on under different circumstances? Or is it a seed that blooms over an extended period of time depending on how much we nurture it?

Growing up in a liberal family with first-generation entrepreneurs, I have had complete mental and creative freedom to envision a career for myself.

There were never any urgent financial demands which required me to give precedence to getting a job and sticking to it. Every time I felt restless within me I asked myself to imagine standing at a crossroad - trying to identify the possible paths available to me and which one should I choose at that particular moment. Thus, by this point of time, with 14+ years of work experience, I have tried everything from a full-time job, multiple part-time jobs, project-based long-term assignments, and freelance work - that too across multi-disciplinary domains.

I kept seeking newer experiences through traveling around the world, undertaking diverse and challenging work assignments, and studying a wide range of courses and personal growth books. I have visited 140+ unknown tiny dots on a map of villages in India, interacted with local communities across diverse conversations on cuisine, heritage, and cultural traditions, and have experienced the true 'Atithi Devo Bhava' (A guest is as sacred as God), that defines our Indian culture.

But still, underneath it all, with a background of high academic qualifications, supportive large extended family, multidisciplinary work experience, and already on my second passport through world travels; I felt like a feather without a cap to belong to. I tried my best to find peace in everyone's belief that I am an intelligent individual with high potential who will achieve great things in life - IF only I would settle down and focus my energies on a well-defined path.

But the inner me, she lived in a constant state of emotional turmoil. I was not unhappy per se but always had a constant soft voice in my head that I have not found my place in the world. At this particular time, I was feeling incomplete in all aspects of life. I was single and wanted to be in a meaningful relationship. I was working hard to lose weight and making slow to no progress. I was working in a high-stress work environment where we were being forced since they did not have the liberty to terminate our position.

And amidst all this negativity, I broke down and went into a shell where I did not get out of my bed, much less my room or house for almost 3 weeks. The only person whom I responded to, one of my best friends for 28 years now, signed me up to go volunteer for a post-disaster mapping of cultural sites in Uttarakhand after the cloudburst in 2013. While everyone was being evacuated,

I took a backpack and blindly signed up to lead a group of students for documentation. Because the one thing that came naturally to me in my quest for self-discovery and freedom was - traveling. And it was here that I experienced a life-changing turn.

The entire space from the Kedarnath temple was ravaged and in a state of destruction. Not just people, animals, and vehicles, but entire hamlets and clusters of villages were washed away with no sign of their existence. When documenting one such site, I came across a middle-aged man looking blank sitting on a stone at the edge of the river. Something about him, made me go strike up a conversation like I had been doing for a week with locals.

When asked why was sitting on a stone alone, his response in a non-emotional tone left a permanent impression on me till today. His entire village, all houses, farms along with his family of wife, mother, and three children had been taken away in the water's flow - he saw them falling away to their death being unable to help. And now he was sitting and waiting for the water to take him away too. No will to eat, drink, move or live. It is an emotion that cannot be expressed in words and my fingers tremble as I even try writing this. But it was one of those moments which snapped me out of the negative, depressing self-victim state I had put myself in.

We all think we have time - but no one knows how much. I promised to get myself back and start building a life based on my hopes instead of my fears. On the way back via Delhi, I got a permanent tattoo that spells 'Wanderlust' on my left wrist. It is to remind me to pick up a haversack and go be anonymous in a new place every time I feel I am losing my individuality. Since then, every year, for at least 3-6 weeks, I go to any remote part of the Himalayas and just give myself the time to reset - to just be.

Since then, it has still been an exploration of where I belong, but with an open and curious mind. I also found the missing core element – that of pursuing an intentional lifestyle. And realized that life's too short to be unhappy, unsure, or unfulfilled. The journey is not over by far, but I know how to identify the crossroads in my life and what to do if I am stuck.

Professionally, I have been part of prestigious projects like the World heritage site management plan for Ellora for UNESCO; headed rural tourism livelihoods for Swades Foundation, Andra Pradesh Government, Madhya Pradesh Government; undertaken research projects for IIT Delhi, documentation of historic stepwells across Gujarat and Madhya Pradesh; a core faculty member for college of architecture and most recently over past three years, undertaken senior leadership roles for MCCIA, Pune City Connect, and Tata Technologies. From heading multiple projects and being in leadership roles, my winsple-most important takeaway is that there is nothing as fulfilling as enabling a self-motivated individual to craft and pursue an intentional life of purpose.

After all, how many moments in life can you point to and say " That's when something changed irrevocably". After all, how many moments in life can you point to and say "That's when something changed irrevocably". One such moment for me was when I read #Amishtripathi words in #OathofVayuputra, specifically the following two lines:

'Shreyaan sva dharmo vigunaha para dharmaat svanushthitat.'

It means that it is better to commit mistakes on the path that one's soul is meant to walk on than to live a perfect life on a path that is not meant for one's soul.

and

Discharge one's own swadharma, personal law, even if tinged with faults, rather than attempt to live a life meant for another.

And it so happens that along with being an entrepreneur's daughter and sister, I am now also a wife to one, invoking a constant comparative analysis being drawn between employment and self-employment. It has, by no means been linear progress nor a very structured one.

It has taken me fourteen years to realize that my professional aspirations lie in a role where my work itself is to make everyone feel like someone who can conquer worlds, especially their world. With that purpose, since 2020, I am a certified Life Coach who helps people stop living on autopilot and craft an intentional lifestyle based on their choices instead of obligations.

And finally, in 2021, I chose to give entrepreneurship my full attention and registered one of my own - Timekeepers Consultants. Our mission is to help professionals double their productivity to accelerate success in the workplace and in life. We work with IT employees, solopreneurs, and students to help them achieve their full potential.

In less than a year, we have worked with corporate clients in the IT industry, healthcare research industry, and IAS aspirants; collaborated with multiple organizations to offer joint training, coaching, and placement programs.

My personal mission - as a coach and as a business - is to help professionals build more fulfilling careers by making their time at work count

CHAPTER NINETEEN

Jaspriya Gandhok

REBORN, ON THE WRONG SIDE OF 40!

Jaspriya Gandhokc

When she was younger (not that she's old but much younger than she is now), she had thought that by the time she will be 50, she will be close to hanging her boots and be ready to lead a relaxed, retired life, having taken care of most of her responsibilities. But, as things stand today, instead of retiring, she is starting her life all over again. And trust me, it is not easy to accomplish if you are on the wrong side of 40. She is 47. This is a story of resilience, indomitable spirit, and self-discovery. This is the story of Jaspriya.

Jaspriya grew up with a normal childhood. Though her family had limited means and had their fair share of challenges, it was a close-knit and loving unit. She was a vivacious child; also, a dreamer. She was an avid reader and reading fuelled her imagination. Being inspired by her mother, she dreamt of being a good mother and raising a warm and loving family, just as her mother had.

But marriage and family were not the only things on her mind, she also wanted to be independent and carve out her identity. After she finished her education, she started working and that's where she met her future husband. Theirs was a whirlwind romance, the stuff that fairytales are made of. After a brief courtship, they were married.

As they settled in their married life, she realized that she faced an extra set of challenges than a regular marriage because theirs was an inter-faith marriage. But over time, they learned to tide over the differences. And life fell into a comfortable rhythm. She continued working for many years after getting married, but as her two children came along, her responsibilities increased. That's when she decided to put her career on hold to focus completely on raising her children, especially her daughter as she had started playing competitive tennis. To support her daughter, Jaspriya had to step into many roles; a chauffeur, a nutritionist, and a travel companion, in addition to all the responsibilities she already had. But she had no complaints. She was happy and content in her small little world – a loving husband, beautiful children, and a warm and cozy home. Life was monotonous, but it was safe and secure. Jaspriya believed that she had found her "Happily Ever After". Unfortunately, it was not so.

After 17 years, Jaspriya's marriage came to an abrupt end. Not going deep into what happened and why it happened, dear reader, for not it is enough to know that her world turned upside down in a matter of moments – it was not a slow death but a single shot in the heart – quick but not clean.

As her world came crashing down, Jaspriya was at a loss for what to do with her life. From one moment to the next, she was in completely uncharted waters, answering an out-of-syllabus question and she was anything but prepared for it. She went into a shock and then, into a downward spiral of self-pity, anxiety, and panic. The world went dark suddenly and there was no light at the end of the tunnel. But as they say, then you touch the rock bottom, the only way out is, up.

Out of nowhere, one morning, when she got out of her bed and saw herself in the morning, Jaspriya could recognize herself. She did not like what she saw and that was the turning point for her. All her life she had wanted to set an example for her children and what she was becoming was definitely what she wanted her children to follow. More importantly, she realized that she owed it to herself that she did not give up on life. The end of a relationship did not mean the end of life – it only meant a change of course.

She decided to take back control of her life and face the challenges head-on. She started by going back to her passion for writing poetry. Writing gave an outlet to her feeling and she started to heal. She realized that to re-enter the professional arena, she will need to upskill herself. She enrolled herself for various certifications and added to her skills. Brick by brick, she started to lay the foundation of her new life.

Jaspriya uses her life story to inspire other women who are stuck in loveless marriages and toxic relationships. She shares the lessons she learned from being in an unhappy marriage and why it is important to end a relationship when it compromises your self-respect and dignity. Here are the three things that she highlights from her experience:

1. **The first lesson is letting go of the victim mentality** – What do we call the people who live through an accident or a calamity? Survivors. So why should we label ourselves as victims when we face setbacks and disappointments. The fact that we are living to see this day, despite all the hardships we have faced or are facing, only reiterates that we are survivors, not victims. Victims don't live to tell their tales. Accept the situation you are in; take responsibility for your circumstances and decide how you want to deal with it. You may have little control over the challenges you face, but you have full control over what you do to handle those challenges. To be a victim or to be a survivor, the choice is always yours.

1. **The second lesson is to build your identity** – reconnect with the person you are when stripped of all the labels you attach to yourself. In our struggle to be the best at all the roles we play, we tend to lose our individuality. Learn to acknowledge and fulfill your needs as a person, and learn to love and nurture yourself. Believe me, all the resources you need to build a meaningful and fulfilling life are all within you. You have to dig deep and get in touch with yourself to tap into those resources. The day you will depend only on yourself for your happiness, you will experience the heavy weight of expectations lift from your shoulders. Only when you feel whole as a person, content and happy, will you be able to spread that happiness around you. Essentially, to live up to all the roles you play, first, you have to be yourself. Always remember, a woman

is much more than the total of her parts and you have to embark on the journey to find that greater whole – the real you!

3. **The third lesson to is find your Ikagai** – Ikagai is a Japanese concept and it means reason for being. To lead an enriching and fulfilling life, you must have a purpose in life, the reason for you to step out of the bed every morning and look forward to what the day holds for you. The purpose of your life must be in sync with the person you are, your true identity. It doesn't have to be grandiose or aimed at the larger good. It can be small, simple, and relevant only to you – but it must be something that brings joy to your heart and meaning to your life. Your life must be spent in pursuit of this purpose and every day to be spent in a way that brings you closer to realizing your Ikagai.

Today, after two years of that life-altering event, Jaspriya has found her purpose. She realized that she would become the guide she once needed tremendously. She is a sought-after life coach and mentor and renowned motivational speaker. Her company mindscapes coaching is a life coaching and self-help company that empowers people with the much-needed guided path that they seek when in dilemma. Mindscapes coaching provides personalized guides to self-development and does not believe in one size fits all, much as Jaspriya. She believes that her real journey in life has started now, as she has stepped out of the different roles she was playing earlier, to become her person. While her destination may not yet be in sight and she has a long way to go, she knows that she will make it one day. This poem written by Jaspriya encapsulates her growing confidence and self-belief.

Find Jaspriya Gandhok and Mindscapes Coaching:
https://www.facebook.com/jaspriya.gandhok
https://www.instagram.com/jaspriyagandhok
https://instagram.com/life_in_post_its
https://www.linkedin.com/in/jaspriyagandhok
https://www.linkedin.com/company/mindscapescoaching
https://www.facebook.com/mindscapescoachingandconsulting

CHAPTER TWENTY

Shobha Managoli

The Power of the Psychological Mind

Shobha Managoli

There is no health without mental health. Taking care of mental health is everybody's responsibility Shobha Managoli is a life coach and mental health professional. In her 30 yrs + of career she has done 85000hrs of therapy and also trained over 300+ mental health professionals in this field. This is a brief of her journey from Shobha the carefree, mischievous, people person to Shobha Managoli the Clinical Psychologist.

"Education is the most powerful weapon which you can use to change the world"- Nelson Mandela. Education that got her here was a Gold medal in BA Hons Psychology in 1985, followed by M.A. in Clinical Psychology in 1987. Pursuing her passion further she joined the esteemed institute NIMHANS for her M.Phil (Medical & Social Psychology) in 1988.

Her professional career started post-NIMHANS in Jodhpur (Rajasthan) as a clinical psychologist in a school for mentally challenged children called Navjyothi Manovikas Kendra and a private practitioner.

The work in the school consisted of educating the parents about the condition of their child and teaching them the techniques to deal with the challenges faced by them, training teachers in handling children and creating IEP's & ITP's as well as coordinating with different doctors like Neurologists and Paediatricians and inviting them to school for health check-ups and awareness programs for parents & teachers.

Her journey as a private practitioner was more challenging and exciting. She started by turning her home into a clinic. Later she joined a polyclinic for consultations so that she can maintain a distance between her home and work.

Her move to Bangalore after establishing 6 years of a successful career in Jodhpur was a huge turning point. Seeing the ample possibilities and opportunities she took a strategic decision to be a diversified practitioner. The person who was instrumental in helping her take the decision was Dr. Ranganathan who advised her saying that "You have a way of doing things and your philosophy should be Reaching the Unreached. Identify populations that have not been reached for mental health services and find a way out to reach them."

She describes herself as a professional who works with target groups –

- Urban to Rural
- Slum to board room
- Paediatric to Geriatric

Her work has received appreciation and awards

• Young Scientist Award from the Indian Academy of Applied Psychology in 1993.

• Jan Seva award -by Yuvachetana Yuvajana Kendra for her contribution to human resources, and many more in 2002.

Since 1997 in Bangalore she has trained budding psychologists, social workers, women leaders, educationists, entrepreneurs, and activists.

She was the Head of Academics and Training for Prism Books Pvt Ltd and had spearheaded the NIE program of The Hindu Newspaper across 13 cities in India.

She has donned many hats of being a Consultant, Curriculum Developer for skills training, Life Coach, Trainer, and of course her passionate role–Therapist and Author.

Amongst the companies and organizations, she has worked with are:

• Jodhpur

○ Navjyothi Manokas Kendra

- ○ Nidan Polyclinic
- ● Bangalore
- ○ KSRTC
- ○ Sudarshan Vidya Mandir
- ○ Infopace Management Pvt. Ltd.
- ○ Prism Books Pvt Ltd
- ○ Swami Vivekanand Youth Movement (SVYM)
- ○ Aikya
- ○ Prerna
- ○ Relationship Experts
- ○ Vee2Care

Currently, she is the Head Parenting Practise at Parentof Solutions Pvt Limited.

Shobha's journey toward success was not easy. In her own words her challenges are:

1. A lack of Support system to set up private practice in India.

2. Lack of supervision or mentoring opportunities post NIMHANS when faced with challenging cases

3. Explaining to people what work I do and how I do it.

4. Explaining to school authorities the role of a school counselor and the way to go forward.

5. In clinical psychology we are taught to deal with individuals, in practice, we have to deal with society and systems.

6. Resistance to refer from the medical fraternity itself.

7. Stigma of going to a psychologist.

She dealt with her personal and professional challenges with grit and determination. That makes Shobha the Professional and Successful Shobha Managoli.

A journey like this cannot be without achievements. Some of her achievements have been:

• First clinical psychologist to establish a private practice in Rajasthan in 1991, without marketing and running a clinic successfully for six years.

• Trained as a Master Trainer in a collaborative project of NCTE & UNPFA on Reproductive Health and HIV/AIDS.

• Training coordinators, and resource persons across 13 cities on 30 thematic modules

○ Focussing on training housewives to deliver the program.

• Being part of the core team for the -Youth Empowerment Sports Department, Government of Karnataka life skills training –Developing the modules and running the pilot project.

• Being part of establishing the De-addiction center for KSRTC.

• Publishing my maiden book–" Powerful Dialogues, A toolkit for Self-Reflection & Transformation."

• My work at Parent of on being the expert for the AI/ML-based app for parents and children–Connecting psychology and technology to democratize skills training and coaching.

Her journey has not stopped. She is still gung-ho about the work she still wants to do. Some of her future plans and ideas are :

1. Tribes of Women: A virtual and offline platform for women to come together and find a safe space for them to express themselves.

2. Mental Health Professional Confluence: A virtual platform and a community for varied Mental Health Professionals to come together, collaborate and learn from each other.

3. Mansik Swasthya Pahal, Let's Talk Mental Health: An initiative at Empowering Educational Institution management principals, academic and non-academic staff on the importance of mental health campaigns in their respective institutions by providing a way to customize and personalize service for each stakeholder of the institution.

4. Magic Tool: A statistical model which can be automated to assess the performance, of the students in the school system and provide a way for Schools & College counselors to make informed choices based on data analysis for creating the counseling plan for the institution.

5. Continue my journey as an author and publish my 2 novellas and a series of short stories.

CHAPTER TWENTY-ONE

Shefali Kumar Jindal

A HEALTHY BODY AND A HEALTHY MIND: THE PERSPECTIVE OF A PSYCHOLOGIST AND NUTRITIONIST

Enter Caption

Dr. Shefali Kumar Jindal is a Registered Dietitian, a Consulting Psychologist, a Certified Diabetes Educator, and a Nutrigenomics who is a PhD in psychology and currently pursuing a PhD in nutrition. She is also a certified Diabetes Educator and a nutrigenomics counselor. Her firm Shefali Kumar's Health Mantr (SKHM) has been providing psychological and dietary counseling to people for more than 10 years. In addition to the counseling, her firm also sells chemical-free dietary, wellness, and beauty products such as protein powders, acidity powders, weight-loss attas, meal replacers, soothing creams, and serums etc. Her firm is also currently developing products for mental health as well. One of her products is a fudge for children with ADHD, which was also her Master's dissertation project. This fudge was tested on underprivileged children with ADHD and showed a great improvement in their learning patterns and attention spans.

Her efforts in developing products for children with special needs is commendable. Her vision of helping people and finding solutions to problems shines through her efforts. Her firm also charts out different nutrition programs like pregnancy diets wherein a diet plan is charted out depending on what trimester the mother and the baby are in since in each trimester the baby's needs are different. In conjunction with that, her firm also offers a plan for postpartum depression which mothers go through after the delivery. This plan is part psychological counseling and part nutritional in nature. The phases of pregnancy and the period post-pregnancy could prove to be some of the most difficult times in a woman's life. Dr. Shefali's understanding of this issue and her solution-oriented approach reflects the kind of person she is. She is definitely a believer in being a problem-solver for people. This attitude of being an outgoing caring person with a knack for helping people through their difficult times, be it physical or mental is what is reflected in her firm's 'mantra': a combination of diet and psychological counseling, clubbing the idea of a healthy mind and a healthy body in one package.

While speaking about the counseling side of things she believes that it is important to seek professional help when it comes to mental health problems and to de-stigmatize mental health problems. It is important to treat mental illnesses at par with physical illnesses as they can impact a person's lifestyle and well-being similar to a physical illness. According to her once a person acknowledges that they are going through some sort of mental distress it becomes the first step they take toward their own mental well-being. Once a person has acknowledged that they are going through something, they can then move on to seeking professional help. According to Dr. Shefali communication is the key to solving our problems. Once we start to communicate and talk openly about what has been affecting us we can put our problems into perspective and begin to let go of the negative emotions that affect us.

The second thing in our plan of action should be to develop a routine. Developing a routine is an important step in the journey of a healthy mind, as a routine gives one purpose, a reason to wake up and look forward to something, it can very well become a way to give meaning to our lives. Dr. Shefali's recommendations are easy to implement in our own lives, her advice to begin with self-introspection and then move towards giving structure to our daily activities might as well be the success 'mantra' we are all looking for.

Speaking of her career as a dietician, she recalls two interesting incidents. Once when a man came to her seeking a plan for weight loss but the caveat being, that he did not want to leave alcohol. He had gone to a lot of dieticians before Dr. Shefali, and all of them had asked him to leave alcohol. He approached Dr. Shefali and requested her to chart out a plan such that his alcohol consumption may not be affected. Dr. Shefali took it up as a challenge because alcohol consumption can pose a difficult challenge to the cause of weight loss as it might lead to one putting on weight. She charted out a diet plan keeping the specific requirements of her client in mind and he had lost around 25kgs in a year. Another incident that she recalls is about a sugar patient, who did not want to start medication.

His blood sugar level was 341 and his HBA1C level was over 11 while the normal range should be around 5. Dr. Shefali took it as another challenge and the plan she brought down the patient's HBA1C to 10.3 within a week. And in 6 months his HBA1C level came down to 5.3 and he had lost 36 kilograms. Dr. Shefali's determination and her expertise as a dietician are reflected in such instances. It was because of her expertise and experience as a dietician she was also invited to work with the CRPF (Central Reserve Police Force). In the session she conducted as part of her workshop, Dr. Shefali gave the CRPF jawans tips on how to maintain a healthy diet and proper nutrition in difficult terrains and during heavy training regimes. She was happy to know that many of her tips and advice regarding the diet of the jawans were then implemented.

Through these anecdotes, we can learn one thing clearly, which is that if we work hard, keep on practicing our skills, keep taking on challenges and learn through them we can definitely achieve some sort of expertise and mastery in that field and as we become masters life will reward us as it has rewarded Dr. Shefali.

Dr. Shefali also talks about her first love and passion which is her love for animals, especially stray animals. She has always been inclined toward providing aid to stray animals. Dr. Shefali even goes on to say that the immense motivation for the success she has found in her career has originated from her dream of being able to open a shelter of her own. Dr. Shefali recalls her days in Nagpur, where she co-founded an organization for stray animals when she was young. She fondly remembers how her organization was full of animal-loving souls who were loyal to the purpose of helping strays. The organization over a span of five to six years would annually organize adoption camps that would provide loving forever homes for more than a hundred stray dogs.

They also made consistent efforts to check on the dogs, their owners, and the environment they were in. The organization was thorough as well as consistent with the counseling of the owners who wished to adopt the dogs. The purpose was to give the dogs a safe and responsible environment in which they could make their home. Her passion and love for stray dogs are commendable. It brings out Dr. Shefali's compassionate nature.

Such has been the life of Dr. Shefali Kumar Jindal. She has helped numerous people along in her journey to lead better lives both physically and mentally. She teaches us the importance of pouring all of your passion into the field you love and how alongside working hard it is important to keep on challenging yourself as it will birth innovation in you. She is also a living example of how all of this is not possible if we do not have a touch of compassion and love for those in the world. And even after accomplishing so much in her life she still says that there is still a lot more she has to achieve and a lot more to learn.

You can connect with her on Instagram, Linkedin, and Facebook via the following links:
Instagram: SKHM99
https://www.facebook.com/ShefaliKumarsHealthMantr/
https://www.linkedin.com/in/dr-shefali-kumar-jindal-0355a81a7

CHAPTER TWENTY-TWO

Roopa Rajan

Nutritional Value of Healthy Food

Roopa Rajan

Food is not rational, food is culture, habit, craving, health, and identity. Roopa Rajan is an entrepreneur, food enthusiast, and recipe developer. She is born to spread love and happiness through food. Roopa was born in Mysore, Karnataka. She completed her school and she complete her B.Sc. in

Psychology in Mysore. After completing her B.Sc., she joined the University of Mysore for her M.Sc. She completed her M.Sc. in Food and Nutrition. From childhood her interest in food and nutrition was extreme.

In Roopa's philosophy, "A healthy gut is the foundation of a healthy mind." She founded Nutrisupa in January 2021. Nutrisupa manufactures Indian Soup products like Moringa lentil soup, Almond fennel soup, and ready-to-use products like Kesar Badam mix. All the products are plant-based, vegan, and natural with no added artificial flavors, preservatives, or colors.

Roopa's inspiration and motivation for making the Indian plant-based vegan food came from her grandmother, mother, and from the various women in Indian culture who make food by using natural Indian spices and local ingredients.

Her keen eye for choosing the best ingredients for her culinary experiments emerged from her childhood visits to the Mysore market with her father. She likes interacting with people and making food for them. In her words, "I love feeding people. I love to see them smile. I love to see people engage in the conversation when they have a meal together."

In a short time, Roopa added many feathers to her Chef's Hat. She was one of the 15 women entrepreneurs in Bangalore, from the F&B segment, to win an entrepreneurship challenge organized by Global Alliance for Mass Entrepreneurship. She has also been on social chef platforms, where she has shared some of her traditional recipes.

CHAPTER TWENTY-THREE

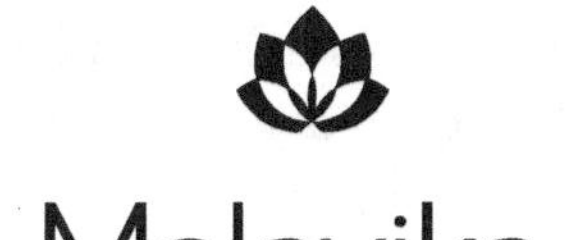

Dr. Malavika Iyer

“When you accept yourself, you’re invincible”

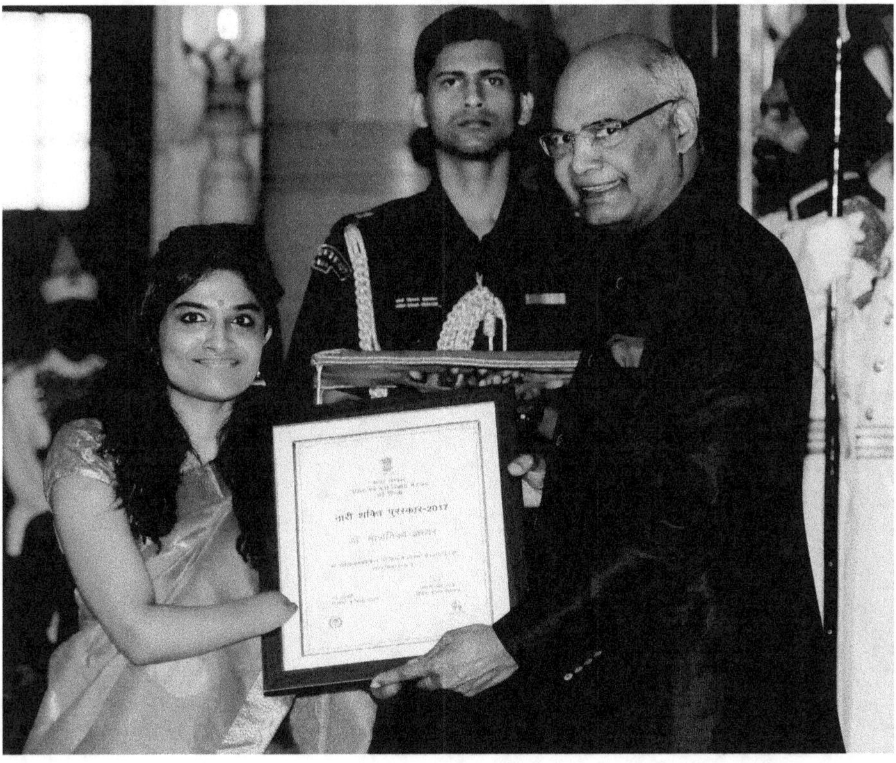

Malavika Iyer

Dr. Malvika Iyer's story is one of courage and determination. She has come a long way from surviving a gruesome bomb blast at the age of 13 that blew off her arms and severely damaged her legs, to winning the highest civilian honor from the President of India. Dr. Iyer has also given talks on related topics at the United Nations in New York City in 2017 earning her a standing ovation, and she served as the youngest co-chair at the World Economic Forum India Economic Summit 2017. Today, she is an international motivational speaker, inspiring millions of people to forget their limitations and take on the world with confidence and hope.

Behind that confidence lies years of struggle with finding herself and practicing self-love. In 2002 in Bikaner, she was a victim of a bomb blast she had lost 80 percent of her blood and doctors said that she wouldn't survive. Yet she did. Even after losing both of her arms and being bed-ridden for over a year her family never made her feel like she was a burden or them or she was differently abled. "All my mom wanted was for me to live; she said she didn't care if I had lost my hands, she would take care of me no matter what."

"Knowing my and my mom's personalities, I would have had a happy life for sure. But the accident, my disability, and my experiences have given me a new perspective towards life, made me humble, and taught me to be content."

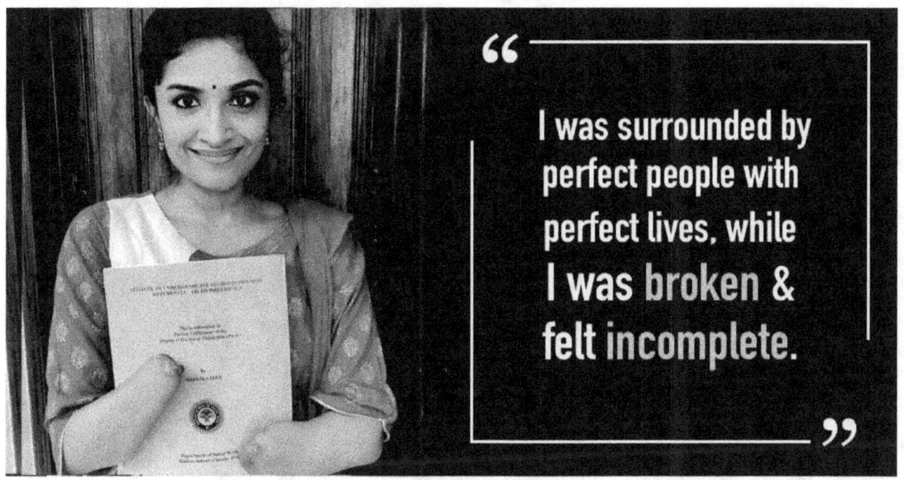

Even though her home environment was more inclusive of her, she did not find the same attitude outside. "Travelling to and between hospitals, I used to get stared at, pitied, and be at the receiving end of insensitive remarks such as 'Bechari ladki', 'She's never going to be able to study', or 'Who will marry her?'. Even when I went back to school and later joined college, I was subjected to curious stares, which brought on feelings of self-doubt and insecurity. At times, dealing with these stares, comments, and emotions was more painful. Growing up as a disabled woman was sort of a double challenge, because of my disability and gender."

Being a victim of discrimination led Dr. Iyer to pursue her doctoral thesis on attitudinal barriers toward people with disabilities. Her aim was to understand the attitude of young people towards those with disabilities, and she interviewed around 1,000 college students in Chennai for it. From her research, she gathered that discriminatory ideas and beliefs start at a young age when individuals come across others different from themselves and find it hard to accept the differences.

Dr. Iyer believes it is all about attitude. When we mold a young mind we need to teach them to be more inclusive and sensitive towards other people.

The focus should be on giving children a wider perspective so that they can see beyond the differences. She recalls 2018 an incident in 2018 when she received the Nari Shakti Puraskar from the President of India. She had received the award and was waiting at the Delhi Airport in a wheelchair.

A group of people came to her right when she was about to board and bombarded her with ugly and insensitive questions. Iyer felt it was unfair to not be recognized for her hard work and to be identified only as a person with a disability because people were not able to see beyond it. It is this change in discriminatory attitudes that she wants to bring about.

"People with disabilities need to be portrayed right by the media – not as a liability, but as a source of inspiration, as individuals who can equally participate in politics, governance, and any field of their choosing."

Dr. Iyer has been a source of inspiration and she doesn't mind being seen in that light but what she really wants is to be acknowledged as an equal, a person who is completely capable of doing whatever she is determined to do, and a person free to make her choices, an individual with an identity of her own which is far beyond her disabilities.

CHAPTER TWENTY-FOUR

Shubhra Chadda

HOW TO CREATE A LIFESTYLE AND SOUVENIR BRAND: SHUBHRA CHADDA AND HER MAGNETIC JOURNEY

Shubhra Chadda

Shubhra Chadda is the co-founder at Chumbak Design, one of India's leading design houses, bringing together a curated mix of clothing accessories and home décor. In 2009 Shubhra Shubhra co-founded Chumbak with her husband, Vivek Prabhakar. Chumbak has come a long way and the story of the founders is truly inspiring. Quirky vibrant products across 100 categories are what make Chumbak a one-of-a-kind brand. As co-founder of one of the biggest lifestyle brands in India, Shubhra has managed to reach heights and has given creativity a whole new level of fabulous.

Chumbak was launched as an India-themed souvenir brand in 2009, with her husband joining her in 2011. She began her lessons in retail marketing and sales. While she hoped to sell her merchandise at airport stores and hotels, she found more enthusiasm among smaller stores that skipped the questions on brand name and margins, focusing exclusively on Chumbak's unique offerings, instead. Within six months of its launch, Chumbak's designs were available in 12 categories such as fridge magnets, sippers, notebooks, keychains, bookmarks, mugs, and cushion covers, across 60 stores and also online.

Shubhra was clear she didn't want Chumbak to be a boutique brand, but rather one that was accessible and affordable to everyone. But finding prominent retail spaces was quite a task. Shubhra recounts how setting up the first pop-up store at one of Bengaluru's biggest malls involved quite a lot of pleading and convincing. Though Chumbak eventually managed to get a 20 sq ft space next to an escalator, Shubhra didn't let the area deter her and designed a fun-filled, colorful kiosk that shoppers simply couldn't resist. And two weeks later, she received a call from the mall manager offering her 150 sq ft on the ground floor for the same price. Within two years, the company turned profitable, and then they were faced with the next step — growth, which required funding.

The couple was clear on the need to take the brand beyond, to launch more products and set up Chumbak's exclusive stores, but were apprehensive on how getting investors in would change things. Everything worked out well in the end when Seedfund's Bharati Jacob, invested $2 million in 2012, put the founders at ease, and reinforced their vision for Chumbak. After that, there was no looking back. Shubhra and her husband took Chumbak forward with their vision and the company has flourished since.

As a woman entrepreneur, she believes that the reason behind a low number of female entrepreneurs is the conditioning of the mind that people then propagate. "A lot of people think it's a man's job. I was fortunate enough to have supportive parents; a lot of women have to go through a number of struggles before taking such a step for their growth," says Shubhra. In her years in the business, she has observed that vendors are more comfortable talking to men and trusting men than women, they feel that a woman always needs a man around and she cannot go on her own. She believes that this is the conditioning that needs to be altered.

As a parent who has a daughter, she realizes how the world can be unsafe and polarizing for women. But she wants her daughter to focus on the positives and says that a change is coming but it is slow, more and more people are recognizing the unfairness in this world.

Parmesh Shahani

IDENTITY AND INDIA: HOW PARMESH SHAHANI IS BRINGING OUT THE CONVERSATIONS OF ACCEPTANCE TO THE PUBLIC

Parmesh Shahani

Parmesh Shahani is an author, public speaker, culture curator, and inclusion advocate. He has had a hyphenated career that has spanned academia, media, and the corporate world, and involved founding India's first youth expression website, editing fashion and lifestyle magazines, setting up a media convergence think tank at MIT, and helping re-imagine the future of two of India's largest business conglomerates through a series of cultural experiments.

He is the author of the book Gay Bombay which was published in 2008. According to him, the book became a useful space for him to look at issues of identity, issues of community, and issues of nationhood. There is still a certain idea of what it means to be a good Indian, and conforming to heteronormative imaginations is very important in that, so this book was also in a way saying that there are multiple ways of being Indian.

The central question the book posed was, in this idea of India can queer people fit into the multiple ways of being Indian? He found quite interesting answers in his book, what he found was the fact that people were really comfortable expressing their sexuality. What the actual concern for them was, how do they frame their sexuality and their identity from what was expected of them? "How do I frame or situate my sexuality in the context of my being a son, a brother, someone who's expected to be married, someone who's Gujarati or Sindhi or Parsi or Muslim or Brahmin?" What he saw was that for most people it was an either/or situation but Parmesh has argued for seeing one's identity as 'and' that is, one's identity as a queer person and their cultural identities can co-exist.

He founded and ran the Godrej India Culture Lab, an award-winning experimental ideas space, from 2011 to 2021. The lab was a unique public space that cross-pollinated people and ideas from across academia, business, and the creative industries to explore the textured nature of Indian modernity. The Lab engaged with multiple audiences via events, installations, screenings, performances, and digital projects. It also conducted student leadership programs and fellowships, produced white papers and mapping resources, and powered collaborations with other national and global cultural institutions.

He also worked on other Godrej projects dealing with human capital and innovation. In 2012, he helped conceive Godrej LOUD, a unique MBA campus recruitment drive that funds the personal dreams of students alongside their internships. From 2014, I served as the curator of the annual Godrej Leadership Forum, a conference for senior management across the Godrej group, and between March 2021 and September 2021, he led the strategic reboot of the group's diversity and inclusion agenda.

Through him being a part of different queer movements he says that he has learned to value multiplicity.

"There are multiple ways of being, and as long as we can recognize that and respect others for their ways of being, I think that's fine. I don't like binaries, center versus periphery. Why can't we all be nodes in a fractal and interconnected network?"

For him, contextualizing the idea of queerness is very important. One cannot look at the west and say that India is years behind or it will follow a similar trajectory. Instead, it is important to focus on the specific context in which the Indian queer movement exists. He says that the Indian queer movement has really learned a lot from queer movements all over the world, but in return, it has also given a lot to queer movements all over the world, so we need to think of movements as an exchange of ideas rather than a one-way flow.

The object of Parmesh involving himself in projects such as the Godrej Culture lab is so that he can bring out these conversations into the public discourse, making it richer, deeper, interconnected, and more meaningful.

CHAPTER TWENTY-SIX

Riya Hemant Gote

SELF-POWER IS SUPERPOWER:

Riya Hemant Gote

Today, a girl who was very motivated to pursue journalism is a business owner. From wanting to be a journalist to being a content writer and getting featured in Forbes magazine was a dream come true for her. Riya was 15 when she decided to be a journalist. Upon pouring her heart out in front of her family, she decided to pursue engineering. Keeping her dreams to herself, she started her engineering course.

Finally, Riya managed to complete her engineering in first class. The four years of engineering were like a nightmare to her. Societal pressure suppressed her dreams and made her emotionally detached from herself.

After her engineering, Riya was firm in traveling abroad and pursuing her Masters. By God's grace and strong willpower, she landed in Singapore to start her management course. She fell. She stood up. She broke. She gathered. She excelled in her master's.

Sadly, her dream to land in a Singapore-based firm broke as soon as the Government announced the changed rules. Being an international student, she had no option but to travel back to her hometown Pune. Completely tensed, Riya was in a dilemma about her career. She had a dream to pursue her Ph.D. in her lifetime. Her professor mentioned that a few years of work experience is required to land in the Ph.D. course.

After working in a Pune-based firm for two months, she quit. She made sure not to land a job and start her venture. This was because the company she worked for had a disaster work culture, and Riya did not belong there.

Today, Riya is glad to be the Founder of Scriberlee, a digital marketing firm based in Pune. How could she figure out how to ascend the stepping stool?

"Elation" is a condition of severe joy and fearlessness. Riya was battling to observe that state was getting hard for Riya when she finished her Masters. She was heartbroken. She was frustrated, upset, and stressed as she condemned herself for not being sufficiently commendable to break the job vacancy in a Singapore-based organization. In the meantime, she composed an article on her Singapore journey and poured her sincere experience on LinkedIn.

We do not have the foggiest idea of how and when life shocks us! When Riya posted this article on LinkedIn, she got a call from an Indian organization saying they preferred her composing style and believed that she should write content for them. As she always wanted to be a journalist, she had a different bundle of affection for composing content. Without taking a minute, she quickly acknowledged the proposition. Although the compensation was more petite, she was partaking in the work offered.

Following a couple of months, the organization designated Riya as a specialist content writer. This supported her certainty, and she began working with various organizations as a "Freelance Content Writer." She was successful in delivering content to homegrown as well as global clients. Yes, she faced rejections and lost a few clients, but she never stopped. Today, she is overpowered to have clients from Canada, Singapore, the UK, and India. She cherishes her work, and she stays by a sincere statement that says, "Never lose trust as you don't have the foggiest idea what opportunities you might get by your activities and actions."

After going through many battles, she characterized joyful life as, "Bliss isn't the shortfall of issues and problems, it is the capacity to manage them."

Toward the beginning of 2020, a famous bank in Africa invited her to be the guest speaker for their syndicated program. This syndicated program made a stage for her as a "Motivational Public Speaker." She acknowledged the proposition and found that she has the potential to be a motivational speaker as well! She joyfully partook as a guest speaker in various worldwide organizations. She had confidence in never losing any opportunity.

With an increase in global clients, Riya established her firm. She named her firm "Scriberlee." "To Scribe" signifies "to write." Being the Founder of Scriberlee, she had the vision to spread her insight and help organizations with branding and marketing services.

Back in 2009, she saw composing and writing as her leisure activity, and individuals around her continued to brush her brain - "You grow up, teach yourself and land in a decent workplace." Somewhere even she was persuaded and decided to be an engineer.

While her Master's, she had a lot of assignments that redeveloped her interest in writing. She started to read more and was enjoying the phase. It is rightly said that life happens to you when you are busy planning other things. But things do not always work according to your plan. IT'S OKAY NOT TO HAVE ONE. She had no intent to be a content writer, but she had a potential that she decided to pursue, and eventually, things started falling in place.

Nothing comes easy in life. She realized this when she had to struggle hard to find the right career for herself. Being the female founder, she had to go through many undecided tests. Society pursues female entrepreneurs as dominating women. She experienced this when her male clients dared to comment on her femininity.

She had no plans of being a content writer. But yes, she had a bumpy start, and she was going with the flow. She had the potential to write, and she cultivated it by making lots of effort. She had to stand firm, fight society, and make her place in the community as a female entrepreneur.

From starting her journey as a freelance content writer to being featured in Forbes to being featured in more than 70 worldwide newspapers as an emerging women entrepreneur, Riya set an example for ladies to follow their dreams. Riya strives hard to spread the message among the women community – "We as women, should stand by our dreams, follow our passion and achieve our goals. Society will perceive whatever they want to. Don't think about what people would think. You are a woman. You deserve whatever you desire."

To do what you love and be successful at it — that's what we're all aiming for. Riya identified her skill as being a content writer. She mastered her skill and turned her talent into a passion. Soon enough, she was on the verge of breaking out and blazing her trail.

It's okay not to be good at one thing because we might be good at the other two. Riya realized this in a complex way: you cannot please everyone, wait for society to accept you, and cannot make everyone happy. But from Riya, it is clear that we can keep ourselves happy by pursuing the career of our choice, which will make us feel proud and happy.

"Self-assurance is a superpower. When you have confidence in yourself, the magic starts happening."

Few lines of Riya to empower every woman –
    Keep shining like the sun ray
    You deserve to smile today
    You are the glittery star
    Study, work, and drive the car

Make yourself proud
    Speak less, and actions are loud
    Run, fall, get up, take care
    No matter what, be strong there

Make happy, proud memories few
    The spotlight is on you
    You are your star
    You have handled yourself so far

Chase your dreams, touch the sky
    You have God's blessings to fly high
    You'll always be your sweetheart
    God has made you a priceless art

CHAPTER TWENTY-SEVEN

Sharmila Divatia

A Born Warrior:

Sharmila Divatia

Sharmila Divatia was born in 1964 in a Gujarati joint family in New Delhi. She started her schooling in New Delhi. Then her family moved to Baroda, Gujarat due to her father's business reason in April 1970. Two months later, she was in a coma and diagnosed with Encephalitis. After one month she lost sensation in her left side eye, voice, hand, and legs. After 15 years of extensive therapy, she gets her body back to the working situation. Though she still has a speech impediment, a spastic left hand, and cerebral palsy as an after-effect of the disease. The Children's Orthopedic Hospital in Haji Ali area was her vacation place to spend her holidays at school time.

Sharmila completes her schooling at Rosary High School in 1988. She was in the science stream. During her school days, she was pretty good academically. At that time, she uses to cycle a lot and played hockey in school. At the same time, she was painfully conscious of her so-called handicaps. That thing turned her into an introvert. But her family stepped in and helped her to overcome the problems. She says "My parents, especially, have made sure that I have a spine of not just bone and cartilage, but of steel."

She completed her Graduation in B.Sc. Mathematics from The Maharaja Sayajirao University of Baroda in 1986. After that, she completed her M.Sc. in Mathematics from the same university in 1988. Another shock was in store for her when she started her job search for a job after completing her post-graduation. She applied to various companies, got interview calls, and got rejected instantly. She didn't lose hope after that, she joined a diploma course at her university. After that, she completed her M.B.A in 1996 from Indira Gandhi National Open University while working at DDE ORG.

After completing her education, she got a job at Silverline Technologies as Software Analyst in April 1996. She worked with them for 7 years till Jul 2003. After she worked with Aegis till April 2015. She also did faculty for 8 years at the University of Mumbai. She is also co-founder of a company called Birngle.

Sharmila has also been involved with a few NGOs in Delhi and Baroda that work for the PwDs and also in the Abilympics (Abilities Olympics) in the country. She was a judge in the regional and national Abilympics held in New Delhi in November 2001 and November 2002 web designing event in internationals in November 2003 and 2007 in New Delhi and Japan respectively.

She was on the governing body of the National Abilympics Association of India and sat on the board of directors of the National Trust for the welfare of people with Autism, Cerebral Palsy, Mental Retardation, and Multiple Disabilities under the aegis of the Ministry of Social Justice and Empowerment, Government of India, New Delhi. Sharmila was appointed a director on another board – ARUNIM [Association for Rehabilitation Under National Trust Initiative of Marketing], also under the National Trust. The inauguration ceremony was held on 22nd September 2008 and was at the hands of Dr. APJ Abdul Kalam. One of her best memories is my meetings with Dr. APJ.

She received many awards and recognition for her inspiring and motivational life journey. Some of them are mentioned below.

1. NASEOH in 2008 for successfully living life despite being disabled.
2. IFUWA ICON: A part of Graduate Women International, Geneva, Aug. 2020.
3. Nav Shakti: A part of BN Patel Institute of Paramedical & Sciences at Anand Gujarat in Oct. 2020.
4. Women Achievers Award by BN Patel Institute of Paramedical & Sciences at Anand, Gujarat in March 2021.
5. Eves Against The Odds – A book curated by Bhavesh Kothari and Hariharan Iyer, Billennium Divas that covers my story as a part of the 25 stories in the book.

How to contact:-
LinkedIn:- https://www.linkedin.com/in/sharmilad
Facebook:- https://www.facebook.com/sharmila.divatia

CHAPTER TWENTY-EIGHT

Rashmi Daga

Satisfy Your Hunger

Rashmi Daga

Some people dream about success, while other people get up every morning and make it possible. Reshmi Daga not just dreams about her success She works hard to make it the reality of her life. Reshmi Daga was born in 1980 in a typical Marwari family. Reshmi's family used to live in a small town called Ramgarh in West Bengal. There were four members in her family. Her mother, father, and her brother. With her family, she shifted to Delhi when she was just 6 years old. The upbringing and love of her family were essential in way of her successful journey.

Swami Vivekananda says "The secret of life is not enjoyment but education through experience." Reshmi's education life was important for making her business life joyful. After finishing school life, she joined the Delhi College of Engineering in 1997. She finished her B.E, Electrical Engineering course in 2001. Then she joined the Indian Institute of Management Ahmedabad for MBA and completed her MBA in 2003.

Entrepreneurship, nevertheless, wasn't the first step for Reshmi. After completing her MBA, she took up a job at IBM through campus recruitment in June 2003. After the first few months of training, she was given a sales manager role, where she learned her greatest life skills. After that, she joined Johnson & Johnson in December 2005 as a regional sales executive. There she experienced working with doctors, chemists, and parents. In December 2007 she left Johnson & Johnson. After that, she gets married and moved to Bangalore with her husband. After moving to Bangalore, she joined a Bangalore-based edtech start-up company TutorVista January 2008.

In 2011, she started her first start-up as Afday.com. It was an e-commerce platform for jewelry, home decoration, and gift articles from artists across the country. After one year Rashmi realized it would not go far. So, she decides to shut down that business. After that, she joined Bluestone an online jewelry store, and worked with them till Oct 2013. After leaving Bluestone she joined OLA in Dec 2013 for 8 months as sales head. Her thought behind working in multiple sectors was, that will make her prepare for a much bigger landscape later. It happened in July 2014.

In 2014 she moved to the food industry with FreshMenu. FreshMenu is an online restaurant that today clocks 14,000 orders per day from its app and website across Bangalore, Mumbai, South Delhi, and Gurugram. And the average order amount is Rs.320. They have 1,800 different food items from different food cuisine. According to Rashmi Daga FreshMenu does everything, from sourcing the ingredient to getting food delivered to the customer's table.

For her impressive work as an entrepreneur, she gets many awards. She was awarded Forty under 40 in 2018 by Et & Spencer Stuart. She gets ET Facebook Women Ahead Award in Aug 2018. As a women entrepreneur, she received Et Prime Women Award in April 2019. In Aug 2019 she received Fortune 40 under 40 by Fortune.

Her journey was not easy. From a sales manager post to a founder of a successful business. In this way, she faced many experiences, good as well as bad. Throughout her journey, in every step, she learned new things. That helps her to achieve the fame of success. So never stop learning, because life never stops teaching.

Santwana Deb

Never stop trying, until it's your last breath

Santwana Deb

It's a story about a simple middle-class girl. The timing was the early 90 her father was a strict teacher in primary school. There were 6 family members in her family. They used live small village called "simul bari". At that time girls are very restricted towards education and other essential daily things. And those times the salary of a primary teacher was not efficient for a 6-member family. They use to get 18,00rs/month. At that salary managing children's education, health care, and house essentials were very challenging. Sometimes they use to cook one's and eat that for 3 times.

She was very sharp in education during her school days. She scored very good marks in her Madhamik exam. She was very closed to her school teachers. They also loved her for her interest towards study. But fortune didn't give her the opportunity. It was the timing before her higher secondary exam. Her grandmother gets very ill. And her family gives her the responsibility of looking after the family's work. She was just 16 but she take all responsibility into her hands. In the higher secondary exam, she manages to score first division.

Not just in education, she was brilliant at singing as well. She never takes any singing education. She started singing beginnings at her school. It was a cultural program at school. Teachers were finding a chorus singer. They found her when she was singing a Rabindra sangeet alone in class after the end of school. She was scared of the stage. But one teacher told her that she will stay behind her while she will perform. That conversation was enough for her to get motivated. After that, in every cultural program, she was the center of attraction for the audience. Due to an unfavorable situation and less supportive family she left her singing talent.

After her school, she started teaching students to continue her higher studies. She was a good teacher. Her mentorship of students was unique. But her luck was not as good as others. When she was in 2nd year of her college, her family fixed her marriage. She wasn't ready for that but at that time she doesn't have any option but to say no. She gets married in the year of 1996.

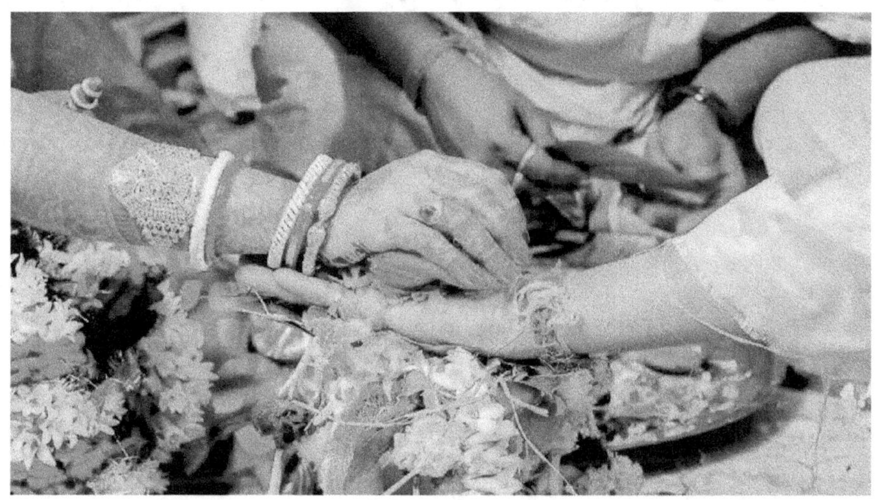

Due to marriage into a big joined family, she gets more responsibility. She becomes everyone's expectations keeper. She was the "boro bou" of that family. Due to over responsibility for her new family, she didn't get any chance to say that she wants to study and find a job.

In that family she wasn't allowed to go out and try to find any preferable job on site she knew that.

❧❧❧

Her love and attachment toward her family were real. Even she forgot to take care of herself. Her first preference was family then her health and dream. Her restless hard work and carelessness for her heath affect her a few years later. After 10 years of marriage life, she gets ill from the death disease Malaria. It takes 2 years for her life to get well again. After 2 years she again gets ill from Tuberculosis(TB). It also takes 2 years of her life to get well again. After 2 big diseases, she becomes weaker in health.

❧❧❧

It's not the end of her struggle life. After 20 years of marriage life, her husband falls into a financial crisis. At that time managing her son's education expenses and family expenses are get impossible for her husband.

That she didn't fall back she decide to jump into a business.

She manages some funding and starts a small Saree stall at her house. That business was not that big but at that time it was important to carry her family's needs.

May she not achieve any big achievements in her life. But what she did in her life that's more than some achievements. One thing that is most inspirational in her life that is, she didn't stop trying and never lose hope. That helps her to overcome her problems. We all need that quality in us. And this is the story of SANTWANA DEB.

CHAPTER THIRTY

Anangsha Alammyan

A writer with the golden pen:

Anangsha Alammyan

Writing is the art of expressing the vision of fictional and nonfictional thoughts. Founding Father of the USA, Benjamin Franklin says- "Either writes something worth reading or do something worth writing about." Anangsha Alammyan did both through her brilliant writing skill. This extremely talented writer was born on 14 October 1991. Anangsha's family used to live in the motherland of Bihu at Assam. We can say in her writing and inspiring life might get that classical calm touch from her born land.

Education is important for making us what we are capable of. Anangsha completed her valuable school life at Jawar Navodaya Vidyalaya in Assam. After that, she joins the National Institute of Technology at Silchar to complete her Bachelor's Degree in Civil Engineering. Her college life was very balanced academically and socially. She was the editor of the college's literary society and dramatic club. In May 2015 she completed her graduation with a department rank of 4.

Then in 2018, she completed her Master's Degree from the Indian Institute of Technology at Guwahati as Geotechnical Engineer. After that started doing her Ph.D. at the same institute. But she dropped out after 3 years. According to Anangsha – "My thesis topic was Seismic response of shallow foundations on the slope was super interesting, no doubt, but I realized the passion to be a full-time writer was burning red hot in my heart. I wanted to give this a chance, and so, here we are." She also worked as Assistant Professor at the National Institute of Technology.

Writing become Anangsha's passion from her reading habit. Her reading journey started when she was three years old and couldn't understand English. Her father used to sit with her and read out Tintin comics. She looked at the illustrations, heard the story in his words, and enjoyed the sessions so much. She couldn't wait to start reading books on her own. She read her first novel when she was ten years old. It was an adventure story by Enid Blyton that kept her hooked. Since then, she has seen reading at least one book each week. Her 3 most favorite books are Arundhati Roy's – "The God of Small Things", Douglas Adam's "The Hitchhiker's Guide to the Galaxy", and Steven Erikson's – "Malazan Book of the Fallen".

As for how she became a writer, she loved writing poems even as a kid and wrote her first poem dedicated to her mother when she was just 5. Anangsha thought of writing novels later in life because she realized there were no books that told the kind of story She wanted to read. There was only one way to solve this: write that novel. She writes 3 books "Stolen Reflections" in 2018, "What did Tashi do?" in 2019, and "What happened to our forever". The first one is a poetry book, 2nd one is a cyber crime thriller, and 3rd one is a romance thriller.

Quora two-time top writer, one of the recognized writers in Medium, Anangsha has 56000+ followers. As a reader, writer, teacher, student, engineer, and freelance writer she inspires everyone towards living life as an expresser or writer.

How to find her:
    Linked In:- https://www.linkedin.com/in/anangsha-alammyan
    YouTube:- https://youtube.com/c/AnangshaAlammyan
    Twitter:- anangsha_

Aishwarya Ashok

Painting is just another way of keeping a diary:

Aishwarya Ashok

According to Pablo Picasso – "Painting is just another way of keeping a diary." Aishwarya Ashok painted her life in such a good way like a diary. She was born in Tamil Nadu in the land of southern India. Her family was a typical south Indian family. They raised her with love & care and with pure

Indian culture & values. Her education started at Chettinad Vidhyashram School. Not just academically she was excellent in culture and sports. She was a member of the dance club and chess club simultaneously. She was a district-level chess player. After leaving that school in 2005, she joined a convent school.

Aishwarya joined convent school, Holy Angels in 2006. She was a school topper in the board exam in class x and a department topper in Higher Secondary Examination in class xii. She was from science. She completed her school life in 2012. Then she joined SSN College of Engineering in 2012. Her Bachelor of Engineering (B.E.) in Electronics and Communications completed in the year 2016. During her college days, she was a two-time merit scholarship holder and silver medallist.

She also did 2 internships during her engineering studies. One with Reliance Communications and the other with Lucas TVS. Those internships teach her the basics of the IT world. In 2019 she starts her work life with Women In Product. She worked with them in the core team of the Indian chapter till October 2021. In 2019 she also joins Havard Business Review as Advisory Council Member.

Aishwarya founded her company TheProdcast in October 2019 in Chennai. The Prodcast is a one-stop platform for indicating and curating product-based stories and conversations. TheProdcast's aim is to empower and encourage product enthusiasts. She is also Product Co-Lead & Marketing Head in LonePack and a Product Mentor at adplist.org. Not just this she also works full-time at Zoho as a Product Manager.

Aishwarya is a passionate work lover who is always ready for the intersection of building, marketing, and transforming products. She is not just a workaholic woman her interest in writing, painting, and reading is extreme. Aishwarya says – "I love writing as much as painting and reading, and certainly wish to retire with some books on one of those seascapes I paint."

How to find her:-
  Linked In:- https://www.linkedin.com/in/aishwarya-ashok
  Website:- http://www.aishashok.com

CHAPTER THIRTY-TWO

Sadhana Jadhav

EXPANDING YOUR HORIZONS OF KNOWLEDGE: WHAT WE CAN LEARN FROM SADHANA JHADHAV'S 25 YEARS OF ERUDITION AND ENTREPRENEURSHIP

Sadhana Jadhav

Ms. Sadhana Jadhav hails from Kalwa city in Thane and is the founder of St. George Education Trust. Her institution conducts various educational and training activities under different banners. She believes in learning and her mantra of self-improvement. She has been picking a new skill every year as a personal and social project. She has a keen interest in learning new things and a plethora of hobbies. Sadhana talks about the struggles in Kalwa where there aren't a sufficient number of resources in the field of education for children, so they have to go to Thane in search of these resources. The problem is that not all parents can send their children to Thane.

This is what motivates Sadhana to learn new things which are to acquire new skills and be a contributing member of the community in Kalwa. In Kalwa, the introduction of subjects such as a foreign language or something in the arts field is not easily available. Sadhana takes up the task to learn these new skills that she can further teach students in Kalwa and they can easily access the learning of all these skills from the comfort of their hometown. Sharing her knowledge gives her immense pleasure and proudly can talk about the achievements of her students who have won various government awards from the Thane Mahanagarpalika.

Sadhana talks about her journey of 25 years and the hard work that has led her to where she is today. She goes back to her roots and talks about her origins in a middle-class family that was unaware of the world of business. The norm of the time was to study and get a job and the fact was that there was discrimination against women in business and it was anyways very difficult to gather the capital to start a business without some sort of a person financially backing your work. Yet, she had decided early on she wanted to be her own boss as she did not want a job to hinder her learning.

She remembers all the obstacles she faced at the beginning of her career which included learning marketing, sales, and how to interact with people, all from scratch and at the root level. She talks about her struggles in learning advertising and printing business cards, etc. Moreover, aNer all these obstacles, Sadhana proudly says that she now helps women start their own businesses and teaches them about the basics such as what licenses to acquire and how to launch their start-ups whether small scale or large scale.

She shares her qualifications including her MBA degree and her national and international certifications. She keeps up with these certifications for her business and is driven by her passion. She gives an example of an interaction with her students where she motivates them to score well by sharing her own experience of learning with them. She takes an example of her students who are studying for IS, UPS, NDA, and students who are doing their masters abroad. Sadhana shares her belief in giving students a holistic education rather than an education that just concentrates on academics.

She encourages her students in extracurriculars such as self-defense sword fighting, sports, arts, life skills, etc. She explains how she and her colleagues have preserved the weapons used by Chhatrapati Shivaji Maharaj in his wars so that she can showcase them to students who cannot visit museums and give them exposure to their culture and history.

Sadhana elaborates on her career as a fingerprint analyst which is a scientific tool to help children find the most suitable careers for them. The results from fingerprint analysis help students choose the courses and boards best fit for them. It also aids in personality and brain assessment in regard to discovering the potential they have in their leN or right brain. This focuses children on their occupation and learning. She further confirms the authenticity of the results of the fingerprint analysis. Soon she is going to provide education based on life skills and experiential learning which is based on fingerprint analysis. She is going to open a preschool in Kalwa on 25th June. Sadhana adds to her achievements by stating that the achievement closest to her heart is the first state award she ever received. Sadhana sheds light on the hardships faced by women entrepreneurs, the biggest being the lack of faith in a woman who is without a man. She shares how people don't take female entrepreneurs seriously and waste their time, energy, and resources.

"The girl can do a business successfully." Sadhana talks about how her family is now very proud of her achievements. Sadhana dedicates her success to the support of her parents, guides, friends, and her teachers.

She humbly thanks her criticizer who keeps her going. Sadhana shares her future plans and talks about her future projects such as branching out to social, cultural, and sports fields along with helping women become independent and overcome hardships in their businesses by providing them consultancy. She is further planning to help people from the transgender community and underprivileged communities get access to education.

Sadhana is an inspiring figure who has for the last 25 years dedicated her life to increasing the access of education and skills in her hometown. As a woman entrepreneur who comes from a humble background with almost no education in the field of business her achievements and her efforts to share what she has learned with other people are commendable.

CHAPTER THIRTY-THREE

Koyel Duttagupta

Something beautiful and constructive is on the horizon

Koyel Duttagupta

After spending hefty 15+ years in corporates and gaining extensive experience in the field of content writing and content management, who would be daring enough to start their venture, that from scratch? Koyel

Duttagupta is the founder of 'Communication Horizon', a start-up that specializes in communication-based solutions for interpersonal and professional relationships. Koyel's brainchild, 'Communication Horizon' has been professionally training people as well as corporates in mastering the art of communication. Her years of experience taught her that her niche, her expertise is communication hence she started a venture imparting her knowledge and experience to those who would be in need.

Along with this, Koyel has also authored an e-book on 'Mindful Communication' titled mindful Communication - Within you for a Better you' which is available on Kindle and has been well-appreciated. Under her brand, she has written a few e-books mostly as guides for Content Writing, Blog Writing, and Public Speaking.

Through her vision and expertise, she has helped many by making them capable of effectively conveying their thoughts and expressions. The offerings of Communication Horizon are highly customized and begin with a free clarity call of 30 minutes. Be it linguistic or behavioral, courses are structured post the call. Then the plans are shared with the clients through which they can get clarity on their training plan and can further add or delete topics based on their requirements. Communication Horizon focuses on transparency and quality and not just on mere enrollments.

Find Koyel and Communication Horizon at...

- Facebook

  https://www.facebook.com/communication.horizon

- Instagram

  https://instagram.com/communication.horizon?igshid=1t3cpprqobsjm

- LinkedIn

https://www.linkedin.com/in/koyel-duttagupta-b7a709b2/
https://www.linkedin.com/company/communication-horizon/?viewAsMember=true

- Website

www.communicationhorizon.com

CHAPTER THIRTY-FOUR

WOMEN ENTREPRENEURS

THE CASE OF SUTA AND ITS PROGRESSIVE PRACTICES

Entrepreneurship has seen a surge in the Indian economy over the last decade. In a growing economy, it is important for enterprises to grow as it creates more opportunities in the market. While we have seen a steady growth in the economy and in the number of entrepreneurs in the country most of them have been men. While women do have entrepreneurial ambitions, they have to often combat cultural stigmas, and a lack of financial capital among other issues in order to establish themselves in the market. It is important for our economy that women enter the market as one study suggests that measures to close the gender gap could lead to a 6.8-percent gain in GDP. Another study estimated that advancing women's equality in India could boost its GDP by $0.7 trillion in 2025 or 16 percent as compared to keeping things as they are. The sixth economic census which was taken in 2013-14 showed that Out of 58.5 million businesses counted by that census, 8.05 million were owned by women, which corresponds to a rate of 13.76 percent of women among the total number of entrepreneurs in India. The low rates of female entrepreneurship are also reflected in its low score in the Index of Women Entrepreneurs where it is ranked 52 out of the 57 countries surveyed.

The low rates of female entrepreneurship are the result of several factors. Firstly, there is an obvious unconscious gender bias within the society which also trickles into the corporate community. Gender biases are usually expressions of our prejudices which are socialized into us through traditions, norms, values, culture, and experience. These biases extend into our working cultures and hence give rise to certain systems within the corporate structure as well. An example of such would be the 'alpha male' or 'bro cultures' which are prevalent in the male-dominant corporate networking systems. These relationships lack empathy and see emotional challenges as weaknesses. Such hyper-masculine attitudes in the industry tend to alienate women rather than make them feel inclusive. This is just one of the examples of the situation of women in the entrepreneurial race.

Despite the difficulties that women face when it comes to realizing their entrepreneurial dreams, it is interesting to note that the women who have made it are more inclined toward starting sustainable and progressive businesses. One such brand which was started by two sisters Sujata and Tanya is SUTA. SUTA is a saree brand that believes in ethical production. The brand is already working towards procuring 100% natural materials, reducing its carbon footprint, and shifting to fully hand-weaved and handcrafted products which would mean more employment for local weavers. SUTA is much more than an e-commerce brand, rather they have carved out a niche for themselves and their journey has not been one without difficulties. The sisters started in 2016, with just the two of them and two weavers, and have in just six years made a brand worth 500 million rupees which partners with more than 14,000 weavers.

"We started off as a brand with just the two of us juggling every possible role by ourselves. It wasn't smooth sailing from the word go, we struggled, learned a lot of things the hard way, and survived through challenges that we did not even imagine until then. The one thing that always drove us through the tough times, right from the beginning, was our vision to make a tangible impact on the artisanal economy and to contribute to a better world to the best of our abilities."

What makes them different from the other brands offering similar products apart from their social agenda and the promise towards ethical production is their marketing. If one looks at their Instagram, the difference becomes apparent. Each piece of clothing tells a story, instead of bombarding the consumer with in-your-face advertising, SUTA appeals to an aesthetic.

Their posts have their muses, the SUTA Queens wearing the clothing accompanied by a story either about the clothing or the muse themselves. Hence giving each piece of clothing a uniqueness of its own.

This intent of creating a unique product that tells a story, combined with a progressive inclusive thought can be seen through their campaign for Navratri in 2020, where they marketed the Sari as a gender-fluid concept. Body positivity, gender stereotypes, and finding strength in difficult times have come to the spotlight and people were able to relate to the campaign while also getting inspired through it. The brand built a campaign that celebrates the colors associated with each day of Navratri along with 9 special people who have had incredible journeys in their lives. Beyond what each color symbolizes, the brand wanted to show how the reflections of every color are within each person and how they play an important role in shaping them. Through colors, the traits of fearlessness, resilience, inner strength, and other such core values were explored. These sarees were worn by men and women alike telling stories of inclusivity and love, hence getting the message across.

SUTA in many ways embodies what a 21st-century entrepreneurial venture should look like. It challenges the rigid hyper-masculine ways of the industry not only because it is run by women but also because of what it stands for Inclusivity and love. This messaging is the antithesis of an industry that excludes women and others who are disempowered and tries to bring them forth by telling the stories of people.